PARTNERS IN MINISTRY

PARTNERS IN MINISTRY: CLERGY AND LAITY

by
Roy W. Trueblood
and
Jackie B. Trueblood

ABINGDON PRESS
Nashville

PARTNERS IN MINISTRY: CLERGY AND LAITY

Copyright © 1999 by Abingdon Press

This book is printed on acid-free paper.

Cataloging-in-Publication data is available from the Library of Congress.

Scripture quotations noted RSV are from the Revised Standard Version of the Bible. Copyright © 1946, 1952, 1971 by the Division of Christian Education of the National Council of Churches of Christ in the USA.

Scripture quotations noted KJV are from the King James Version of the Bible.

Scripture quotations noted NCV are from The Holy Bible, New Century Version, copyright © 1987, 1988, 1991 by Word Publishing, Dallas, Texas 75039. Used by permission.

99 00 01 02 03 04 05 06 07 08—10 9 8 7 6 5 4 3 2 1

MANUFACTURED IN THE UNITED STATES OF AMERICA

This book is dedicated to Paul R. Ervin Jr., our first partner in ministry. Paul has walked each step of this journey of faith with us, and to him we express our appreciation for his love, encouragement, and belief in us and in this ministry.

CONTENTS

Partners in Ministry began as a dream. We wondered if anyone else would see what we saw, that with high-quality training in leadership, communication, and team-building skills, clergy and laity could work as teams to more effectively fulfill the mission of the church.

It was with some trepidation that we shared our dream with Bishop Ernest Fitzgerald, who was then the Episcopal leader of the North Georgia Annual Conference of the United Methodist Church. Bishop Fitzgerald saw the possibilities immediately. At the same time Paul Ervin, who was North Georgia Annual Conference Lay Leader, and Rubin Perry, Associate Annual Conference Lay Leader, started encouraging us because they, too, saw the possibilities. We began to experiment with Bishop Fitzgerald and his cabinet.

Paul Ervin was instrumental in helping us lead the College of Bishops for the Southeastern Jurisdiction and their annual conference lay leaders in a Partners in Ministry retreat. From that retreat several bishops and lay leaders caught the vision.

Paul Ervin was again instrumental in getting me before the annual gathering of the National Association of Annual Conference Lay Leaders in both 1993 and 1995. Here the idea of Partners in Ministry (PIM) really caught fire. Many of these lay leaders went back to their annual conferences and urged their bishops, cabinets, district lay leaders, and conference councils to get involved in PIM.

In 1995 we held the first two and one-half day skill training workshop at Lake Junaluska, North Carolina. Dr. Gordon Goodgame, director of Lake Junaluska Assembly, helped make this possible. We were joined in this project by our good friend and colleague Tim Moss from the Board of Discipleship. Four annual conferences were involved in this pilot session, one of which was Southwest Texas.

Under the leadership of Bishop Owen and Martha Etter, Annual Conference Lay Leader, the Southwest Texas team took the ball and ran with it so that today that Annual Conference is still the front-runner. Through Martha's influence other conferences have embraced PIM: Missouri East, Northwest Texas, New Mexico, Western Pennsylvania, Peninsula-Delaware, South Indiana, Virginia, West Virginia, and South Georgia. This list could go on, and we know we have possibly overlooked many who have encouraged and supported us. Our loving intention, though, is to acknowledge all who have made this ministry possible.

We offer a special thanks to the Southeastern Jurisdiction Association of Annual Conference Lay Leaders of the United Methodist Church who sent us unsolicited seed money to get this book started. We appreciate this expression of faith in us and belief in what we feel we have been called to do for our Lord.

Also, we acknowledge The Atlanta Consulting Group—our former partners and associates and the dedicated staff—who for more than seventeen years helped us develop these skills and teach them to Fortune 1000 companies across this country and internationally. We will forever be grateful for the lessons we learned through this association.

So, "the cloud the size of a man's hand" is growing and promises showers of blessing on the church. To God be the glory. Amen.

PREFACE

There is an awakening enthusiasm for making disciples of Jesus Christ in The United Methodist Church today. Leadership will be critical to carry Christ's Church forward in this awakening. United Methodism recognizes every church member as a potential leader. "Partners in Ministry" is resourcing the current leadership, as well as potential leadership for both clergy and laity in a working partnership to create more effective church ministry.

The Conference Board of Laity brought this two and one-half day training program into the Southwest Texas Conference. Over eighty churches have begun to work together toward common visions/goals. Participants in "Partners in Ministry" are taught to "live by the HEART principles." They are trained on how to turn win-lose situations into win-win solutions.

Dr. Roy Trueblood, a noted United Methodist clergy member, developed this program in consultation with colleagues, universities, and the business world. He has trained thirty-two clergy and laity "trainers" in the Southwest Texas Conference. Local congregations have turned a vital corner with members feeling good about the church, where it is going, and what it is doing for Jesus Christ.

I commend this book highly as a proven resource for a more spiritually dynamic and effective local church. I also thank Dr. and Mrs. Trueblood for making this valuable tool available to the larger church. It will make a notable difference in the vitality of any local congregation that desires to become a more convincing witness of what the church is all about.

> Ray Owen
> Resident Bishop
> San Antonio Area
> Rio Grande and Southwest
>   Texas Conferences

INTRODUCTION

This book is written out of love for the church, where congregations have nurtured us all our lives. We have been saved by Christ and redeemed by the love (sometimes *tough* love) of countless laymen and laywomen, pastors, and teachers. So, this book is an offering. We hope to give back in some small measure for all the church has meant to us.

The theme of this book is leadership; we outline and expand on what we believe to be the skills necessary for effective leadership within the church today. This is not to say that leadership in the past has not been effective; it has. It is our belief that some changes can be made to enable present and future leaders within the church to be even more effective.

It is time for changes to be made and new models to be created for ministry. Change is inevitable. However, during the past thirty years change has occurred at a dizzying pace in every area of our lives. A severe drop in membership and giving has occurred in our own and other major denominations within the Christian tradition. At the same time moral behavior and attitudes have sunk to a low ebb, challenging our traditional values. Technology has allowed us instant awareness of what is going on in the world. We have been exposed to weaknesses and flaws in the character of many of our national leaders resulting in an erosion of respect for leadership in every area, including church leaders. This growing cynicism has led many into aberrant forms of worship, even following charismatic gurus to commit mass suicide. Through the media we are constantly being exposed to various forms of idolatry, be it sex, money, fitness, materialism, hedonism. Our churches are filled with idol (idle?) worshipers.

As church leaders we need to make some positive changes, not simply react to current conditions. First of all, we must be clear about and affirm what will never change; that is, the mission and message of the church, which is the same as it was when Jesus gave his disciples their commission. We are to preach the good news that Jesus Christ was and is the Son of God who died on a cross so that we may experience forgiveness, regeneration, and hope for this life and into eternity. We have access to the power of the Holy Spirit to strengthen us in our quest to live like Jesus in an evil world, to resist the temptation to slip into idolatry, and to call us back if and/or when we do fall.

The mission of the church is the same for every Christian and every congregation. How we go about fulfilling our mission must be open to change. We need to look at changing our systems, structures, and leadership behavior not simply because change may be in vogue, but also to be more effective for our Lord and our calling.

We are excited because we see a new day dawning for the church. There is a noticeable awakening, especially on the part of the laity. Laity are growing restless and are more willing now than they have been for some time to engage in ministry. They long for a way to serve their church. They are ready to roll up their sleeves to help the clergy provide leadership for the church.

Laity see the concept of Partners in Ministry as a way to revitalize the church and regain some of the vigor the church displayed in eighteenth century England. Wesley had to rely on lay persons for leadership. He organized them, taught them, sent them out, and reviewed their performance. That partnership and mutual dependence created a tremendously vital movement, which had an unmistakable impact on the culture of Wesley's day.

God is not through with the people called Christians. We still have a message that needs to be heard. The lost and alienated in our culture need to hear the good news of forgiveness and hope for a better life. The poor, homeless, and needy on our streets need our help. The mission of the church today calls for all the resources we can muster.

Partners in Ministry enables clergy and laity to work together to provide the necessary leadership needed now. It is not a new or unique idea. However, as it is presented here, it is practical and useful. The success of this movement has been demonstrated throughout our country.

This book describes what Partners in Ministry is as we understand it. It shows the process by which clergy and laity can become partners and effective leadership team members in every congregation. Our vision is that every congregation will have an opportunity to develop the skills necessary to work effectively as a team, as partners in ministry.

What makes Partners in Ministry so different, special, or unique? First of all, consider the underlying assumptions.

Assumptions

1. All baptized Christians are called into ministry.
2. There are no levels of leadership in the church, only different functions depending upon personal gifts and graces, the call of God, and the confirmation of the church.
3. To be effective, laity and clergy need to work as teams in every local situation and abide by an agreed-upon set of covenants or ground rules for behavior.
4. In order to fulfill assumption number two, clergy and laity need to receive skill training in how to live by the ground rules; and they need to receive this training together.

Covenants and Ground Rules

Partners in Ministry advocates the following set of covenants or ground rules:

1. All team members are committed to Jesus Christ and to a shared vision for the church.
2. All team members agree to live by the **HEART** principles:

   - **H**ear and understand me.
   - **E**ven if you disagree, please don't make me wrong.
   - **A**cknowledge the greatness within me.
   - **R**emember to look for my loving intentions.
   - **T**ell me the truth with compassion.

3. All team members seek win-win solutions to problems, conflicts, or any other issues that arise.
4. All team members keep their agreements and are open and honest in their communications.
5. All team members assume 100 percent responsibility for the results that are produced and do not engage in blaming and justifying.

These assumptions and covenants, or ground rules, are not in themselves unique. Other voices in the church have been advocating these for some time. Many church leaders recognize that clergy and laity must work together in new ways and that laity must find means (other than just by serving on a committee) to use their gifts in ministry with integrity and accountability.

Partners in Ministry provides training in the *skills* necessary to live by the ground rules advocated. In addition this training is unique in the way it is delivered. Participants *practice* the skills *and receive feedback within the workshop.* Not only are thoughts and attitudes changed, but also behavior. Participants learn not only *what* they need to do to be more effective team members, but also *how* to do it. They receive help in implementing the basic principles of PIM in their lives together back home, wherever that may be. And the skills of PIM are provided in a short and easily assimilated and applied manner.

We believe Partners in Ministry has the potential to train and develop a new leadership style that is needed in the church. It is not all that is needed, but it is an essential part. We do need to change some of our structures and systems, but these changes will only come about when leaders trust one another and are willing to listen to one another, to confront one another constructively, to seek win-win solutions to problems and issues, and to give helpful feedback to one another. This is what Partners in Ministry is all about. This new leadership style will then allow us to bring the essential tenets of our faith to a more focused and confident *laos* who then can go into the mission culture in which we now live to carry out the Great Commission.

CHAPTER 1

Vision

Embedded in ground rule #1, *"All team members are committed to Jesus Christ and to a shared vision for the church,"* are some serious implications. First, leadership team members in each congregation need to be chosen carefully. They should be persons of integrity who have demonstrated credibility and have a good reputation with other members of the church and within the community. The leadership team members should have an unquestionable love for Jesus Christ evidenced by faithfulness to their vows of membership in the church.

Leadership team members need to have leadership ability and be willing to dedicate their time and energy to the church. We emphasize this because we have observed that the nominating process in each church does not always result in these kinds of persons in leadership positions. Sometimes the positions are filled by those who succumb to "arm twisting" or who have nothing better to do with their time. Often persons are chosen for leadership positions because they are popular in the community or occupy positions of power and prestige. They may be wealthy persons selected in the hope that by becoming more active in the church more of that wealth may find its way to the offering plate!

We are simply saying that those in positions of nominating others for leadership roles in the church need to approach their task carefully, thoughtfully, and prayerfully. Remember, Jesus spent the night alone in prayer before selecting the twelve special disciples (Luke 6:12-16). The early church, when faced with the task of replacing Judas, chose two men carefully and prayerfully asked God to show them the right person as they cast lots to decide. The apostles were very particular when choosing stewards from among the followers of Jesus in Jerusalem as the church

experienced tremendous growth. Consider their require-
ments—persons of good reputation who were full of faith,
full of wisdom, and, most important, full of the Holy Spirit
(Acts 6:3). Choosing leaders to serve the congregation is a
serious and important task.

Another important implication involves support of the vision
of the church. As we will see in what follows, a clear, shared
vision is crucial for the success of the mission of the church. If
a congregation has no clear vision, then the first major task of
the leadership team is to create one. Team members must
value the importance of vision and invest the necessary time
and energy in developing a vision for the congregation.

If a congregation has an established vision, each team member must be willing to support that vision wholeheartedly. This
is not to say visions never change. They do from time to time
because local situations change. As leaders, we must always
be looking for ways to be more effective and successful in carrying out the work of the church. However, the vision belongs
to the congregation, and leaders need to be in support of the
vision and constantly keep it in front of the people. The leadership team members are stewards, or keepers, of the vision.
So, as we select leaders, we need to know of their commitment to and support of the vision of the church.

Vision is the driving force in any successful organization.
Consider the diagram below:

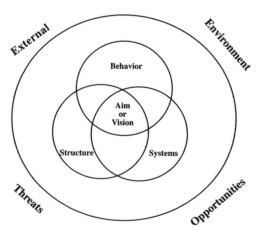

As the diagram indicates, we can look at structures, systems, behavior, and vision. Like the game of pick-up sticks, change in any of these areas has an impact on the other areas because they are all interlocking. At the heart of any effective organization, though, is a meaningful and inspiring vision. Each congregation must have a clear vision or they will continue to produce a variation of what they have been doing year after year. If we always do what we have always done, we will always get what we have always gotten!

Vision changes everything. It dictates systems, structure, and behavior. It provides the "why" of everything we do within the church. Vision is different from mission. Every congregation has the same mission given by Jesus to make disciples. How a congregation goes about fulfilling that mission is the vision. Vision is a picture of a preferred future. What would it look like if we were fulfilling our mission perfectly in our community or parish? That picture is the vision. In what follows we will share more fully our understanding of vision and the visionary process.

Vision has always played a vital role in the history of the church and recently has been rediscovered. A clear vision is a source of power and inspiration. It gives direction and provides motivation. It encourages goal-setting and acknowledges achievement and progress toward the vision. An engaging vision unites and aligns persons and calls them to move in the same direction.

Since this emphasis is so important, we need to be sure we have some common and shared understandings of what vision and visionings are all about. What is "vision"? What does the term mean? How or why does vision "work"? What are the characteristics of an effective vision? Once a vision is established, then what? What do we do? What are the differences between individual vision and corporate or organizational vision? Are there particular pitfalls to be aware of and avoid? Where are the roadblocks? How do we keep our vision alive and vital? These are some of the issues to be addressed in this chapter. The goal is to provide some common understandings and encourage meaningful dialogue.

Some may affirm that the church and each of us as disciples already have a vision given to us by God through Jesus Christ. Jesus calls us to a life of perfection, or perfect love. He has commissioned us to make disciples of all nations and establish the kingdom of God on earth. This is certainly a vision with a stretch! However, we must go on to translate the visionary call of Christ into specific terms where each of us lives and works. We share a common call, but we live under different circumstances. Each congregation is unique, and so we must develop a unique vision for each parish, which will allow us to "bloom where we are planted."

What does "vision" mean? What is "vision"? In Scripture, particularly prophetic literature, it is often seen as a supernatural gift that enables one to see into the future and predict coming events. Sometimes visions come in dreams and reveal unique insights and understanding of current events. We understand vision to be a description of a preferred future—what we want to see happen, not what we already know is going to happen.

You and I are unique in all of God's creation. He has endowed us with special powers. We can look backward through memory and look forward through imagination. When we use the power of imagination, we can be creative and bring into reality what existed before only in our minds. Creation starts with vision. It is a mental picture of a preferred future state. It asks the questions: What do we love? What do we deeply care about? What do we want with our whole hearts? Our vision is the "pearl of great price," the treasure hidden in a field about which Jesus spoke (Matthew 13:44-46). This distinguishes a vision from a dream. A dream says, "Wouldn't it be nice if?" A vision says, "God willing, this *will* come to pass."

We all have the capacity to envision, to shape the future. The ability to create and vision is an integral and essential

20

part of being human. It is a special gift available to all of us. Psalm 8:3-6 (RSV) says, "When I look at thy heavens, the work of thy fingers, the moon and the stars which thou hast established; what is man that thou art mindful of him, and the son of man that thou dost care for him? Yet thou hast made him little less than God, and dost crown him with glory and honor. Thou hast given him dominion over the works of thy hands; thou hast put all things under his feet. . . ." I believe God calls upon all of us to use this gift he has given us. It is essential to a meaningful, purposeful life.

We often quote Proverbs 29:18 (KJV), "Where there is no vision, the people perish. . . ." In his book *Making the Future Work,* John Diebold makes this insightful commentary:

> Far from being merely an abstract or supernatural concept, the idea behind the much-quoted phrase is a down-to-earth observation. It says that human beings need purpose—individually and collectively. Without a sense of purpose the individual is not only lost but will rapidly disintegrate. Without purpose there is no motivation, no direction, no way to focus the physical and mental faculties of the human. What is true of the individual is even more true of the collective, be it the tribe, the nation, the corporation, the union. What holds the body politic together is the communality of purpose. When we say "vision," however, we mean more than a commitment to do now what must be done now. Vision implies a purpose beyond the moment, a view of the future, a dreaming and thinking ahead. A vision suggests the imaginative conceptualization of a future that is not inconsistent with the present but will move the present to something nearer to the ideal.

With this creative gift, God has also given us freedom. We are not compelled to be creative, but the divine tug at our soul is always there and difficult to ignore even when we do not understand it.

It was as if a great bell called to me, far away, a light to the far-away lights in the marsh, saying, "follow . . ." and I know that the truth, the real truth, is there, there just beyond my grasp, if only I can follow it and find it there and tear away that veil which shrouds it . . . it is there if only I can reach it. . . . Lancelot

How does vision "work"? One of the major functions of vision is to provide a clear and compelling sense of direction. We know where we are going, where we are headed. It keeps us from "getting on our horse and riding off in all directions." It focuses our energy and gives us a basis upon which to make critical decisions. Charles Lindbergh had a vision of crossing the Atlantic Ocean by air. He knew that weight would be a critical factor and refused an offer of $1,000 to carry a few ounces of mail with him to Paris.

In the great classic *Alice's Adventures in Wonderland* (Bantam, 1981) Lewis Carroll provides an insightful view into the importance of knowing your destination—having a vision of your direction when undertaking a journey. Alice finds herself in what might quite fairly be described as a highly turbulent environment. She has just escaped from the Duchess who had ordered that Alice's head be chopped off, when she comes upon a cat in a tree:

> The cat only grinned when she saw Alice. It looked good-natured, she thought; still it had very long claws and a great many teeth, so she felt that it had to be treated with respect.
>
> "Cheshire-puss," she began, rather timidly, as she did not at all know whether it would like the name; however, it only grinned a little wider. "Come it's pleased so far," thought Alice, and she went on. "Would you tell me, please, which way I ought to go from here?"
>
> "That depends a good deal on where you want to get to," said the cat.
>
> "I don't much care where—" said Alice.
>
> "Then it doesn't matter which way you go," said the cat.

Just as our vision must be clear, so must our grasp of current reality be firm and objective. The difference between current reality and our vision creates the dynamic or creative tension that produces action leading us toward our vision or may force us to abandon our vision and settle for some version of current reality. Our destination may be clear; but if we do not know where we are, how can we decide which way to go?

This point has been illustrated by William J. O'Brien, president of Hanover Insurance, in his efforts to develop the thinking of the managers within his company. In a management bulletin, O'Brien points out:

> Effective managers know the importance of having a vision of what the group (company, local branch, or department) wants to achieve compared with the present reality of the group's accomplishments.

> One way to picture this is to stretch a rubber band vertically between your hands. The lower end of the band represents the present reality; the upper end represents the vision of what the group wants to achieve. Between the two ends is the tension on the rubber band.

> When the tension is too severe, the rubber band breaks. So, too, in an organization of people if the vision is too far removed from the present reality as seen by the group, the tension may become so great that it is counterproductive. But no tension or too little tension—visions that are not stretching—results in a flaccid organization. Healthy tension is highly desirable.

> If the stretched rubber band represents the tensions created by the distance separating our vision from the present reality, there are two ways to reduce this tension. One, lower the vision; two, raise the level of present reality.

In our churches, agreement on current reality is very important. We can spend countless, fruitless hours arguing about current problems, issues, and challenges that face us.

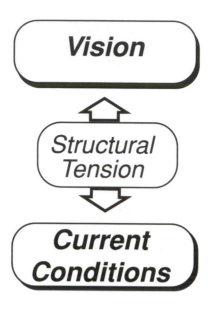

(Management Bulletin, Series XIII, No. 10, June 19, 1984; The American Group)

Once we agree on current conditions, then we can begin strategizing and develop plans to move us from where we are to where we want to be. It was only after the Hebrews finally gave up on the notion that being in slavery in Egypt was better than wandering around in the wilderness that they began to make progress toward the promised land.

What are some of the characteristics of an effective vision? In visioning, as in many areas of life, clarity is power. The most effective visions, the ones that result in creative action, are clear. We can see the preferred future. We can describe it. We can place ourselves in that future and experience it.

Our biblical forebears could do this. They envisioned a promised land, a land of milk and honey, a place they could call their own after many generations of slavery. Sometimes, as with the prophets Daniel and Ezekiel, that future could be fearful and awesome. A vision can be positive and attractive or negative; that is, something to avoid at all costs. Read again the Revelation of John. He knew how to create a word picture of the future in terms his readers could understand, even experience in their imagination (Chapter 21). This clear picture of a heavenly home for eternity allowed the early Christians to endure hardship and persecution. A great vision is so vivid it can produce the sensations of touching, tasting, feeling, seeing, and hearing.

Jesus taught in parables, or word pictures, so that his hearers could "envision" and understand (Matthew 13:34). He also taught us in his great prayer to say, "Thy kingdom come, Thy will be done, on earth as it is in heaven" (Matthew 13:34). What would our earth, our world, be like if everyone acknowledged God as Father and obeyed his commandment to love one another? It would be heaven on earth! Later, he would point the disciples toward the future: "Go therefore and make disciples of all nations, baptizing them in the name of the Father and of the Son and of the Holy Spirit, teaching them to observe all that I have commanded you; and lo, I am with you always, to the close of the age" (Matthew 28:18-20 RSV). Paul, in his vision, later saw Gentiles hearing and believing the Word of God. He saw what eventually happened—the whole world turned upside down for Christ.

Martin Luther King Jr. had a dream; and that dream was very specific. He saw a world where the color of one's skin made no difference. All children would grow up together in peace and harmony. Everyone would have access to education and opportunities to grow and develop their unique potential. He saw from the mountaintop a new world and saw that world in detail.

A great vision is clear and specific. It can be verbally described or written down. It can capture the imagination. A great vision is also moving. It can cause us to laugh, cry, shout, dance, get excited. For a vision to be effective in creating a different future, it must be compelling and motivating. We must want it with our whole heart. Nothing less will do.

One of the reasons why vision statements often do not

produce the desired results is because they are too vague or fail to enroll the emotions. It is easier to give up in the face of difficulties if there is no emotional involvement. If you have a vision for yourself, your family, your church, does it "stir you up"? Does it bring a smile to your face? When you state your vision, is your response, "Yes!"? Does it move you to action? A dull vision will not create dramatic results any more than a wet match can light a fire.

An effective vision is an affirmation in the present tense. It describes the future as though it were already present. This helps create the tension that will move us forward. In the 1980 Winter Olympic games, Billy Johnson looked at the mountain and declared, "This hill is mine." He went on to become the first American to ever win a gold medal in downhill skiing.

A great vision affirmed in the present tense compels us to live "in-tensionally." We either keep moving toward our preferred future or settle for some version of current reality. We cannot stand still. In the Declaration of Independence our forefathers wrote, "We hold these truths to be self-evident, that all men are created equal." They declared a belief to be reality and then acted upon that belief. A great vision is a statement of faith as if it were fact. It is "the *substance* of things *hoped for,* the *evidence* of things *not seen"* (Hebrews 11:1 KJV). In our vision we claim the future as having already happened.

This may be hard to understand, and others learning of our vision may scoff and point out that it does not conform to current reality. So, it takes courage to claim your vision in the face of doubt. It may even be slightly embarrassing at times and we may feel vulnerable. Peter Block in *The Empowered Manager* states, "If your vision statement sounds like motherhood and apple pie and is somewhat embarrassing, you are on the right track." Just remember—it is the tension that creates movement.

All these characteristics of effective visions are the same whether the vision is an individual one or an organizational one. It is interesting to note that when Paul referred to the church, he used the term "Body of Christ." The diverse mem-

26

bers of the church are called to live as one body and share a common vision. However, for a vision to be effective in the church, there are special factors that must be considered.

To bring about personal commitment to an organizational vision requires a careful enrollment process. The vision must be "owned" by each member. This transformation is not easy. There is always the possibility for the uncommitted to claim that it wasn't their vision in the first place.

Visions are typically created by a leader or a small group of leaders. Great visions are not democratic, or created by the masses, but they must reflect the hopes and dreams of all. Inspirational leaders are always ready to give a "stump speech." They share the vision at every opportunity. They are not salespersons. The goal is not to sell, but to enroll, to invite persons to sign on voluntarily. At the end of that hot summer in 1776, after weeks of debate, our founding fathers went forward and individually signed the Declaration of Independence. They enrolled themselves in the vision.

We need to be honest and recognize that not everyone will enroll and even those who do so will possess varying degrees of emotional excitement and commitment. As leaders, we sometimes spend an inordinate amount of time trying to enroll the resisters in our churches and neglect those enrollees who are ready to move on. The following diagram depicts the usual organization and member responses to the vision:

Enrollment Curve

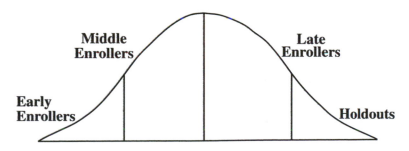

Though the holdouts may never enroll, we must not ignore them. They need to be invited to join in, and they need to know that the church is going to move forward with or without them. This truth must be spoken in love.

A vision alone, even accompanied by strong emotion, is not enough to result in creation. Successful creative results are always accompanied by careful planning, persistence, and hard work—a willingness to do whatever it takes. How does the saying go? "Success is 10 percent inspiration and 90 percent perspiration." Visioning and planning go hand in hand. I saw a poster recently that stated, "A vision without a plan is a dream. A plan without a dream is drudgery. A vision with a plan is humanity's hope for a better world." Or, as Bennis and Nanus (1985) state in their book, *Leaders,* "Vision animates, inspires, transforms purposes into action."

It is important that members be sensitive to one another and support and encourage one another, particularly the leader. The people of Israel looked to Moses for leadership and inspiration. When they saw him standing on the mountain with his arms raised in victory, they fought on with faith and enthusiasm. When Moses was tired and allowed his arms to sag, the people lost heart and began to lose the battle. Seeing this, his aides went to Moses and helped him hold his arms up (Exodus 17:8-13). We play an important role in supporting one another and our leaders.

Progress toward the vision is seldom in a straight line. We often get detoured and sometimes pushed off course by circumstances. Expect setbacks. During these times, it is especially important to affirm the vision, "stay the course," and, as soon as possible, get back on track. We also must see setbacks for what they are. Setbacks test our resolve. Detours are an inconvenience, but they do not keep us from reaching our destination. A sailboat makes headway into the wind only by tacking, but always staying on course. Don't listen to those who say, "I told you it would never work." "Give up now and cut your losses." It is difficult to live in the tension between what is and what will be. Only the discipline of staying on course will allow us to move closer to the vision. If the apostle Paul had allowed all the setbacks to stop him, we would have no church today. It is how we handle the setbacks that makes the difference between moving forward and giving up. We must constantly encourage and support one another in good times as well as bad.

Since there is usually a large gap between current reality and our vision, we must remember to celebrate small victories along the way. As each milestone is reached, we celebrate to keep the desire burning in our hearts. It has been said that an elephant can be eaten one bite at a time; also we can realize our vision one victory at a time. So, we must be aware of and sensitive to victories as they occur.

All of us, young and old, have been created by God with the capacity to see visions and dream dreams. And, for whatever reasons, God has called us to be cocreators in establishing his kingdom on earth. He has given us his Son, the pattern for our personal lives. On the cross, Christ has broken the power of sin and death. He has promised to empower us through the Holy Spirit living within our hearts. He has proclaimed that even the gates of hell shall not prevail against us—that all things are possible (Matthew 16:18).

At some point, we will be called upon to answer for our actions. On Judgment Day we will be asked to report on what we have done with our capacity to envision and create the future. What have we done with his power and inspiration? Will we bury these talents and gifts in the ground, hug the earth, be evaluated by the temporal benefits current reality has to offer? Or, will we assume our role as children of God called upon to envision and create the future as God intends? God will not leave himself without a witness. Can he depend on us or must he look for another?

Summary

What Is a Vision?

- It is a preferred future—a complete picture, written down, visualized.
- It is not simply a goal or a mission statement.
- It is exciting and inspiring.
- It is a gift from the Holy Spirit, and it is unifying (Acts 2:1, 17).
- It is more than a hope, a wish, or a dream. It is a reality waiting to be created.
- It is something we want with all our hearts.
- All that exists now was once in the mind of God or of human beings. Vision is the inspiration for creation.

How Does It Work?

- The gap between what is and what we want to be creates tension. The tension seeks relief. We either move toward the vision or we give up and remain content with some version of current reality. Picture the Hebrews at the bank of the Red Sea. They could move forward to seek the promised land, or they could go back to Egypt and remain slaves. They could not stand in place. They had to go forward or go back.
- The path to a vision is not easy. There will be challenges and temptations to give up. We persevere because the Holy Spirit inspires, strengthens, and encourages us. Hardships drive us to our knees *together*.
- It works because we affirm it. We state our vision in the present tense. It is a done deed.

How Do We Get a Vision?

- We pray.
- We dream.
- We talk.

- We listen.
- We write.
- We revise.
- When we get it, we rejoice and share it every day, everywhere, with everyone.

Heart Principles Inventory

On the following pages are twenty-five descriptive statements about various relationship-building behaviors. Please read each statement carefully; then rate yourself in terms of how frequently you engage in the behavior or action described. Record your responses by drawing a circle around the number that corresponds to the frequency you have selected. You are given five choices.

1. If you *rarely* or *never* do what is described in the statement, circle the number one.
2. If you do what is described *once in a while,* circle the number two.
3. If you *sometimes* do what is described, circle the number three.
4. If you do what is described *fairly often,* circle the number four.
5. If you do what is described *very frequently* or *always,* circle the number five.

In selecting your answer, be realistic about the extent to which you actually engage in each behavior. Do *not* answer in terms of how you would like to see yourself or in terms of what you *should* be doing. Answer in terms of how you typically behave. For example, the first statement is, "I create opportunities for people to talk to me." If you believe you do this *rarely,* circle the number one. If you believe you do this *fairly often,* circle the number four.

Heart Principles Inventory

To what extent do you engage in the following actions and behaviors when interacting with others? Circle the number that applies to each statement.

1	2	3	4	5
Rarely	Once in a While	Sometimes	Fairly Often	Very Frequently

1. I create opportunities for people to talk to me.

   1   2   3   4   5

2. I listen with an open mind to the ideas of others even when I disagree.

   1   2   3   4   5

3. I find ways to help other people utilize their strengths and abilities.

   1   2   3   4   5

4. I make an effort to identify the positive intentions of others when they disagree with me.

   1   2   3   4   5

5. I make my expectations clear when requesting changes in behavior.

   1   2   3   4   5

6. I give 100 percent of my attention during conversations with other people.

   1   2   3   4   5

7. I clearly communicate that my disagreement is with the issue or idea, not with the person.

   1   2   3   4   5

8. I praise people for their contributions and qualities regardless of how large or small.

   1   2   3   4   5

9. I assume the other person has positive intentions and try to understand them when things go wrong.

   1   2   3   4   5

10. I give specific feedback about unsatisfactory behavior in a caring way.

    1   2   3   4   5

11. I show I am interested in what people say by listening carefully and responding to their comments.

    1   2   3   4   5

12. I avoid "putting down" another person when I disagree.

    1   2   3   4   5

13. I point out unique, positive qualities I see in people, even if they do not see them in themselves.

    1   2   3   4   5

14. I ask others about their possible good intentions when I don't know what they are, rather than assuming the worst.

    1   2   3   4   5

15. I indicate how the negative behavior of others will affect our relationship.

    1   2   3   4   5

16. I check for understanding of what others say by summarizing in my own words what has been said.

    1   2   3   4   5

17. I make a point of using language that is not critical or judgmental when I disagree.

    1   2   3   4   5

18. I take the time to find ways of building the self-esteem and self-confidence of others.

    1   2   3   4   5

19. I let others know that I believe in their good intentions when we have different points of view.

    1   2   3   4   5

20. I clarify with the other person their willingness to discuss difficult issues that affect us both.

    1   2   3   4   5

21. I allow other persons equal time to air their views when discussing difficult issues with them.

    1   2   3   4   5

22. I treat others with respect, even if I disagree with their views.

    1   2   3   4   5

23. I let others know that I am comfortable with my own special attributes.

    1   2   3   4   5

24. I acknowledge the helpful intentions of others, even during difficult discussions and confrontations.

    1   2   3   4   5

25. I take responsibility for stating my case when I want someone to change their behavior.

    1   2   3   4   5

CHAPTER 2

Leading from the Heart

The second major covenant or ground rule for clergy and laity leadership teams is, *"All team members agree to live by the* HEART *principles."* Leading from the heart means every member is sensitive to the feelings, needs, desires, and ideas of the others. It means responding lovingly and positively to the unspoken requests we make of one another:

- **H**ear and understand me.
- **E**ven if you disagree, please don't make me wrong.
- **A**cknowledge the greatness within me.
- **R**emember to look for my loving intentions.
- **T**ell me the truth with compassion.

Leading from the heart means allowing the Holy Spirit to govern our behavior in relationships. As the apostle Paul affirmed in Romans 5:5 (RSV), "God's love has been poured into our hearts through the Holy Spirit which has been given to us." Our task as Christian leaders is to allow that love to flow from our hearts to others in very specific behavior.

The heart has always been a powerful symbol in biblical literature. It is the seat of the self, the person within known only to God and to ourselves. We see, as did Samuel, only the outward appearance (1 Samuel 16:7 RSV). God looks upon the heart. Since we cannot look into another's heart, we are left to draw our conclusions based on the way that person behaves toward us and others. As Jesus said, "By their fruits you shall know them." Our hearts can be "deceitful above all things" or the home of the Holy Spirit.

Those whose hearts are not filled with the Holy Spirit tend to behave in selfish and self-centered ways. Before Lee Atwater died of brain cancer, he became a repentant, new-born believer. Before his conversion he had been a brutal, consummate political strategist and hardball Republican National Committee chair. Atwater said, "I acquired more wealth, power, and prestige than most. But you can acquire all you want and still feel empty. It took a deadly disease to put me eye-to-eye with the truth." "But," he said, "it is a truth which this country, caught up in its ruthless ambitions and moral decay, can learn from my dime . . . what's missing in society is what was missing in me . . . heart!"

We cannot lead from the heart as we are defining it here unless our hearts have been renewed and renovated. Self and all the baggage that goes with it must be moved out so that we can make room for the Holy Spirit. When this happens, we are ready to lead from the heart.

More specifically, leading from the heart means responding positively to the five unspoken requests listed above.

Hear and Understand Me

The first unspoken request others make of us is, *"Hear and understand me."* We all have something to say. We have thoughts, feelings, and ideas we want to express; and we want someone to listen. We also have hopes, dreams, fears, and questions we want to express; but who will listen and try to understand us—who we are?

We are born with ears to hear, but we must learn how to listen. Unfortunately, few of us are ever taught how to listen. Jesus said on several occasions, "He who has ears to hear, let him hear." He was saying, in effect, "Don't let this message go in one ear and out the other." I remember as a fourth grader in elementary school having my hearing tested. I passed the test, so the assumption was made that I could then listen. What an assumption! I have spent the rest of my life attempting to hear and understand others, and it isn't always easy.

Listening carefully and thoughtfully to another takes effort and skill. Few have been taught the skill of effective listening. First of all, it is an active process, not a passive one. Just because we hear the sound waves vibrating on the bones of our inner ear does not mean we understand the message being sent. Numerous tests have shown how little of the message we receive is really understood. We must learn not only to listen to words being spoken, but also to "read between the lines." What is implied in the message? It is also important to pay attention to body language, tone of voice, and choice of words.

Most of all, we need to learn how to give evidence to the other person that we not only hear, but that we also understand. Just saying, "I understand," or "I know what you mean," is not enough. It is more effective in communicating understanding to respond with a listening check or a restatement of the message to see if we really do understand. This restatement is very important. First it encourages the speaker by giving evidence that we are listening and attempting to understand. If the restatement indicates to the other that we do really understand, it is extremely gratifying. Now they know they have found someone who will listen. If in the restatement we indicate we have not yet understood, it gives the other person an opportunity to clarify and not continue assuming we know what they mean.

Another way to give evidence of our effort to listen and understand is the open-ended question. This allows the other person to expand on what is being said to help us understand the message. It is important in effective listening to stay on target and not lead the other into areas we would like to talk about to satisfy our own curiosity. It is also important not to make premature assumptions or interpretations of what is being said.

So, listening takes effort; and just to complicate the situation, there are always barriers to effective listening we must overcome. Environmental factors often get in the way— external noise, other conversations, activity going on around us. Think how hard it would be to carry on a meaningful conversation on the floor of the New York Stock Exchange.

We also must resist our own prejudices and our tendency to make judgments or jump to conclusions.

One of the major barriers to listening for understanding is our tendency to think ahead about what we want to say in response. We think much faster than a person can speak, so our brains want to be doing something other than focusing on what is being said. If we are not careful, we may even interrupt the person talking and take control of the conversation in order to talk about ourselves or another topic about which we have more interest. Proverbs 18:13 (NCV) says, "Anyone who answers without listening is foolish and confused." It is interesting to observe how most conversations are people taking turns talking. Any real listening for understanding is purely coincidental!

Jesus is our greatest example and teacher when it comes to listening and being sensitive to what is in the hearts of others. In John 4:6, Jesus, tired by his journey to Samaria, sat down beside a well. When a Samaritan woman came by, he asked her to draw some water for him to drink. During their ensuing conversation, her life was changed. She was so emboldened that she ran back to the village and told everyone she met about Jesus. They came to the well, and their lives were changed, too. What happened in that conversation? The woman summed it up by saying, "Here is a man who told me all that I ever did." Would it be stretching it too far to interpret this as "Finally, I discovered someone who truly understood me—all about me—and loves and accepts me anyway!"? Isn't this the good news we all have discovered in Jesus?

I am convinced the people who flocked around Jesus came not only to hear his teachings, but also to be with someone who listened to them and understood their condition. When Jesus ate and drank with sinners, more than food was exchanged. Jesus listened and understood and shared the good news of the Kingdom and lives were changed. They found someone who understood. I wish I could have been at the table in Zacchaeus's house that evening as he entertained Jesus. We don't know what was said, but we do know Zacchaeus was transformed (Luke 19:1-10).

Listening to another and giving evidence that we are listening is perceived as caring and loving. The poet John Fox wrote, "When someone deeply listens to you, it is like holding out a dented cup you've had since childhood and watching it fill up with cold, fresh water. When it balances on top of the brim, you are understood. When it overflows and touches your skin, you are loved." We don't even need to say, "I love you," or "I care for you." When we listen, the other person can sense it. Listening to one another helps bind us together. One of my favorite thoughts, which has been attributed to George Eliot, says it well. "Oh, the comfort, the inexpressible comfort of feeling safe with a person, having neither to weigh thoughts nor measure words but to pour them all out just as they are, chaff and grain together, knowing that a faithful hand will take and sift them, keep what is worth keeping, and then, with the breath of kindness, blow the rest away."

Since communication is two-way, it is important to take some responsibility as a speaker also. The desire of our heart is to be heard and understood. Jesus spoke in parables to make it easier for people to understand. There are ways we can help those who are listening to us. First, speak in paragraphs and not chapters. It is difficult to listen to a long speech and understand all of it. Use language the other person understands. Avoid a lot of jargon or phrases such as, "You know what I mean." Most of the time they don't; they're listening in order to understand what you mean, so don't short-circuit the process. Try not to ramble. Stay focused on one topic at a time. Give the other person ample opportunity to respond before going on. In these ways we encourage and help others listen to us. Always express appreciation to those who have taken the time and made the effort to listen. Listening for understanding is a gift we can give one another.

In summary, as we seek to work together as partners in

ministry, each member of the team must covenant with the other members to live by the first HEART principle: Hear and understand me. Practice active listening in your deliberations. Give evidence to one another that you are indeed listening and trying to understand. This behavior will help bind you together as a team.

Even if You Disagree, Please Don't Make Me Wrong

The unspoken request, "Hear and understand me," does not require that we agree with what we hear. So, the next HEART principle is, *"Even if you disagree, please don't make me wrong."*

All of us have had the experience of being "put down," embarrassed, or belittled at some point in our lives. To be ridiculed is a powerful blow to our self-esteem. I have often heard people say, "Oh, I can't sing!" when, as a matter of fact, they can. But someone, at some time, laughed at them and told them they could not sing. They believed that negative feedback and from that time forward gave up any attempt to sing.

It is so easy to be critical of one another because we have had a great deal of experience. We have heard negative messages all our lives. We typically are not attracted to put-down artists; on the contrary, we try to avoid them at all costs. So, if we wish to develop positive relationships with others, we need to learn how to practice HEART principle number two. Listen, understand, then agree or disagree; but make a distinction between the person and their ideas, thoughts, proposals, or points of view.

To disagree without making the other person wrong is an important and difficult skill. However, if we can learn to do this, we can keep lines of communication open. "Make wrongs" produces defensiveness and can lead to a win-lose situation. We all like to be right and "win" arguments. If the other person is made to feel like a loser, we may have damaged our relationship, sometimes permanently. Being right is often the booby prize. A former colleague of ours made this point by remarking, "I won every argument I ever had with my ex-wife!" Make-wrong behavior leaves losers in its wake.

Within the church today we are faced with some serious challenges that put this HEART principle to a severe test. How do you feel about abortion, for instance? Can you listen to another point of view without becoming judgmental? What about the issue of homosexuality? What is your position on homosexuals in leadership positions within the church? Can you listen to an opposing view without making wrong those who disagree? The only way we can maintain an opportunity to influence others is to disagree with a position while affirming the person. A seminary professor of historical theology was fond of saying (of various theologians), "The man is much better than his theology."

Jesus is our great example with regard to this HEART principle. The religious leaders of his day were constantly putting him down and seeking opportunities to make him wrong and embarrass him publicly. One attempt is recorded in John 8. A woman taken in the very act of adultery was brought to Jesus to see how he would respond. Instead of doing what the religious leaders wanted, passing judgment on the woman, Jesus challenged them instead. He helped them see how hypocritical it was to judge and sentence this woman when their own hearts were filled with wickedness. "He that is without sin among you, let him first cast a stone at her" (John 8:7 KJV). Jesus challenges us today to do the same sort of introspection. Then he went on to make the important distinction between sin and the sinner. Addressing the woman, he said, "Neither do I condemn thee: go, and sin no more" (John 8:11 KJV). Certainly Jesus was opposed to adultery and disagreed with her behavior; but at the same time, he accepted her as a precious child of God who deserved another chance.

43

As partners in ministry, we are bound to disagree with one another from time to time. We should value different points of view because they can lead to synergistic solutions. The key is to keep our covenant to disagree without making one another wrong. Also, we need to keep in mind that voting among team members should be one of the last options chosen to make important decisions. Every time a vote is taken and it is not unanimous, we create losers. Far better among team members is to take the time and invest the energy in reaching consensus.

Acknowledge the Greatness Within Me

One of the five HEART principles is the unspoken request made by ourselves and others in our relationships with one another, *"Acknowledge the greatness within me."* Some may object to the use of the word *greatness*. However, if we believe our birth was no accident and that God has a purpose for our lives, it is not unreasonable to assume potential greatness in every child of God. We do not mean greatness as the media use the term. We do not have in mind popular sports or political heroes or special geniuses in any field. We are simply affirming that God grants each of us gifts and graces to enable us to do his will and fulfill his purpose in and through our lives. We serve a great God, have a great calling to fulfill, and are granted special talents and abilities. We do have greatness and seeds of greatness that can be nurtured, and each member of the family of God is called upon to nurture the greatness we see in one another.

Nurturing and affirming one another is part of the work of the church and is a responsibility of every Christian. When we baptize our children, the entire congregation vows to help raise these children in the strength and admonition of the Lord. As in the parable of the sower, seeds of greatness in our children must be nurtured, or they may shrivel and die for lack of affirmation. Persons may lose faith in them-selves by having been put down too often. Persons who lack a sense of self-worth do not believe they have any greatness. Or they may have taken some risks and failed and then decided not to try again. Whatever the case, greatness, especially in the young, is fragile.

Acknowledging greatness means that we look for the good in one another and affirm it. Look for small things to acknowledge—an insightful comment, hard work on a spe-cial project, faithful attendance at meetings, promptness, generosity. Wherever we see someone demonstrate any of the fruits of the Spirit, let them know we notice and appre-ciate what they have done. This is especially important with-in our families. Linda Eyre gives some good examples of how her children have expressed their appreciation to fam-ily members in some of the letters they have written over the years. Her seven-year-old daughter told her mom in a Valentine's Day card: "I like the way you take care of me when I am sick or sad or even mad. I am so glad that I came onto this earth with my family. I really do appreciate your doing all that stuff for me and all my brothers and sisters and my dad" (*I Didn't Plan to Be a Witch and Other Surprises of a Joyful Mother* [New York: Simon and Schuster, 1996, p. 179]).

It feels good to be acknowledged. We are attracted to people who notice and comment positively on our behav-ior. It is a bonding behavior that is essential among team members who are working together as partners in ministry. It is easier to hear and accept negative feedback if we have received a generous helping of positive feedback as well.

Criticism is easy. We live in a negative, red check mark world. We grow accustomed to hearing what is wrong with us so that when someone acknowledges our greatness, it often comes as a shock, albeit a pleasant one. We can help one another grow in grace and bond our relationships by affirming one another on a regular basis.

Notice how Jesus looked for and affirmed the greatness

he saw in others. When he looked at Simon, he saw a rock, a leader of the church in the making. Simon Peter never forgot the faith his Lord had in him. And Jesus never gave up on him. Jesus saw the potential in a young man named Nathaniel who on the surface demonstrated only cynicism. Jesus ate and drank with sinners and associated with prostitutes, not because he approved of the behavior, but to affirm their potential greatness as children of a loving and forgiving heavenly Father. He saw a disciple hidden inside a tax collector, Matthew, and a big heart inside a tiny man, Zacchaeus. People flocked around Jesus not simply to hear good sermons, but also to soak up the love and affirmations he constantly extended. And he calls us to do the same today.

We can also help ourselves maintain a healthy sense of self-worth by following these principles:

- Learn to accept yourself just as you are, warts and all.
- Affirm your God-given talents and abilities.
- Allow others to affirm your greatness.
- Affirm the greatness you see in others.
- Eliminate negatives from your life.

First, learn to accept yourself. This is often very difficult for many of us. We have learned since childhood to please other people (parents, teachers, peers, family, etc.) in order to be accepted and, thus, to feel worthwhile. In this case, the locus of self-acceptance is outside of us, invested in others. The challenge is to bring the measurement of our self-worth inside. Our understanding and acceptance of the grace of God make this possible. If God truly accepts us just as we are, who are we to refuse to do so? If we refuse to accept ourselves, we are saying, in effect, that we know better than God. It is evidence that we have not understood or been able to accept God's unconditional love. It is often easier to believe in our heads than to accept in our hearts that God loves us completely without our having to do anything to earn that love. As a friend of ours said, "The heart of the problem is the problem of the heart." Until we are able by the grace of God to accept ourselves just as we are, we cannot proceed to the other steps toward self-acceptance.

Once we have been able to truly accept ourselves, then we can look for and affirm our talents and abilities. Jesus told a parable about servants who were granted "talents." The bottom line is: If God grants you talents, use them for his glory. Even the servant who was granted only one talent was expected to produce results, not bury the talent in the ground.

Take time to inventory your strengths from time to time. Are you using all of them? Have you been neglecting an ability you could be exercising in service as a disciple? Affirming your own greatness is not bragging or being boastful. First of all, you are doing this for your own benefit to develop and maintain your sense of self-worth, not to publish your assessment to the world. Second, remember you can love others to the extent you love yourself. We typically achieve to the level we feel we are worth. To be of greater service to God and others we must become aware of what we have to offer.

The apostle Paul is a good example for us at this point. He was an extremely talented person but did not go around boasting about his abilities or accomplishments. Whatever he was able to do was done through the power of the Holy Spirit. As he said, "I can do all things in him who strengthens me (Philippians 4:13 RSV)." He never failed to give Christ the glory. However, he was aware of his unique talents and abilities so that when challenged he could readily respond (1 Corinthians 11:22-29). So be willing to acknowledge to yourself the gifts you have received from God. Rejoice and be glad.

Another step in the process of developing and maintaining your sense of self-worth is to learn to value the affirmations you receive from others. This may sound strange, but our experience shows that many find it difficult to accept compliments. They discount them, give reasons why they do not fully deserve the compliment, and, in effect, say to the one seeking to affirm them, "You don't really understand. If you really knew me, you wouldn't be saying those kind words." Have you ever found yourself in this position when given a compliment? Do you sometimes feel embarrassed when given a compliment? Why is this? Why do we seem more comfortable looking at our weaknesses than our strengths? For one thing, it challenges the low sense of self-esteem with which many have become comfortable. It may also be perceived as a challenge to live up to the positive expectations of others, and what if we fail? For these and many other reasons, we may find it difficult to receive affirmations from others.

Consider this—An affirmation from another is a gift. Like any gift, if we tell the giver we really don't deserve the gift and then toss it away, the giver certainly will not be motivated to acknowledge us in the future. If we discount the gift, we also discount the giver and cut off a supply we need to grow and develop. If you find yourself uncomfortable in receiving acknowledgment, just see that as a sign that you need to work on this area of your life. Practice seeing yourself as a plant left on the window while the family went off on a two-week vacation. On their return the plant is promptly watered. Try to imagine how that plant must feel (if it has feelings)! We all need to be affirmed regularly if we are to grow and blossom, and we need to learn to soak up affirmations of others and say, "Thank you."

It may seem like a paradox to say that another way to help ourselves with our sense of self-worth is to acknowledge others. Yet any time you spend building up someone else results in your feeling good about yourself. This is what we call the boomerang effect. The biblical principle is the Golden Rule. Jesus also stated, "Give, and it shall be given unto you" (Luke 6:38 KJV). Certainly, we do not give in order to receive, but often we do receive in return. However, if you constantly hand out thorns, don't expect roses in return. If you hand out roses, there is no guarantee you will receive roses in return, but it certainly ups the probability! It is a good and necessary thing in the church to build one another up. This is especially true for team members who must work closely together sharing hardships and joys, taking risks, remaining faithful.

Finally, it is important to eliminate as much of the negative from our lives as we can. The old adage about computers is true for each of us as well—garbage in, garbage out. We live in a negative world, and there are many influences on our lives we cannot control. By the same token, we may have more control than we think; and from time to time, we need to "weed the garden." If you have friends who tend to drag you down, you may want to consider spending less time with them. You have probably heard that some people light up a room when they enter, and others light it up when they leave! If you have a choice, choose to be with the former and avoid the latter. Take an inventory of the books you read and the movies and television programs you watch. Do the clubs to which you belong have a noble purpose or are they a waste of time? All these and other areas of your life may need to come under scrutiny. If these experiences do not offer a positive experience for you, it may be time to look for other activities. Remember, you are doing all this to develop and maintain your self-worth.

We all live in a cage, the bars of which are the ways we have learned to think about ourselves. We need to rattle the cage, move the bars, break out. We can do more for God with a positive sense of self than a negative one. If we have more self-confidence, others will like to be around us, seek us out, and desire to work with us. We will have more influence and present a positive witness to and for others.

Working on yourself is one of the most important things you can do, and to do so is not selfish. Remember that others are counting on you. Christ is counting on you. Your other partners in ministry are counting on you. You do have greatness within you. Do not "hide it under a bushel."

Remember the HEART principle *"Acknowledge the greatness within me."* Look for ways to acknowledge others, especially your leadership team members. Keep your own sense of self-worth at a high level by following the five steps listed above.

Remember to Look for My Loving Intentions

The fourth HEART principle states, *"Remember to look for my loving intentions."* On the surface this may seem like the simplest and easiest of the five HEART principles. However, it may be one of the most difficult to practice. Others often disappoint us by not living up to our expectations or by failing to produce the results they promised. Our knee-jerk reaction is to be critical, complain, or react with negative emotion. For one who has indeed tried and done their best, this negative criticism hurts. We feel punished unjustly. We are treated as though we meant to fail or disappoint when in reality we meant just the opposite. So, if we are to live by this principle, we must pause before being critical of another's performance and ask ourselves, "Did they intend these results? If they had a positive or loving intention for doing what they did, what might it have been?" Good intentions do not always produce good results, but intentions are important. Even though good intentions do not equal good results and we may be unhappy with the results, it is good to affirm the intention.

I have a friend who related that when his two daughters were small, they would often talk, play, and giggle when they were sent to bed to sleep. One night after reminding them a few times of the objective of being put to bed, he heard a crash coming not from their bedroom, but from his. Determined to set things straight, he proceeded down the hall to the bedroom. As he did so, one of the girls came running toward him, nightgown flapping in her wake, and jumped into his arms and pitifully exclaimed, "Oh, Daddy, when I climbed up on the dresser to kiss your picture good night, I knocked the lamp over!"

As one of the authors, I must confess an insensitivity to special days observed by so many. I usually remember birthdays and anniversaries, but beyond that I'm nearly oblivious. I am especially likely to ignore Valentine's Day altogether. Jackie, my wife and coauthor, is just the opposite. She remembers birthdays, anniversaries, and other special days by sending cards to many of her friends and family members. She seldom forgets. She has been working on me with little success for almost twenty years. At least I now feel guilty when I forget!

I have been working especially hard on Valentine's Day because I know she will have a card for me and perhaps even a gift. A couple of years ago on Valentine's Day I remembered to buy a card for her. I rushed to the drugstore only to find the cards had been picked over fairly well. (Oh, before I forget, I seldom spend time trying to find a card with a verse that is appropriate for a specific person. Needless to say, Jackie does. She will spend several minutes in a card shop looking for just the right card.) Meanwhile, back at the drugstore, I found a beautiful card standing alone on the shelf. I was in luck and being rewarded for remembering. On the front the card said, "To My Loving Wife." That was appropriate enough for me. When I reached the checkout counter, I thought I had discovered the reason this card had not previously been selected. It cost $4.50! I experienced sticker shock, but I gulped and bought it. I signed it, put her name on the envelope, and discreetly placed it on the dining room table and waited—quite satisfied with myself—until she discovered it.

When Jackie found the card, she smiled and opened it. As she read the message, she began laughing. I was puzzled because it was not a funny card, but a serious one. I asked her why she was laughing, and she asked in return a tough question, "Did you read this card before you bought it?" For just a second I tried to appear hurt and offended, but then I had to confess what she already knew, "Not all of it." Then

51

she handed it to me. Sure enough—on the top of the page it said, "To My Loving Wife." But at the bottom of the page it read, "On our first Valentine's Day together." Well, since we had been together for eighteen years at that time, I was caught with no place to hide.

Jackie had every right to read the riot act to me. I was guilty. I deserved it. But then she did a wonderful thing. She put her arms around me, gave me a big hug, and said, "Thank you." She recognized my loving intentions. That felt so good.

The fourth HEART principle, when observed, can help others feel a little better when they fail or mess up unintentionally. Most of us are our own worst critics. When we do not live up to expectations, we are usually very hard on ourselves and do not need any more punishment from others. It is especially important to practice this principle with our partners in ministry. Every team member is committed to doing his or her very best. We must assume this and support their loving intentions.

Now this principle says, "Remember to *look for* my loving intentions." This should apply in all our relationships. But it is possible to come across persons who have evil intentions. We must recognize these, too. And if this is the case, we may be called upon to confront this destructive behavior.

One of the great values of forming a leadership team in the local church that practices the covenants defined in this book is that it provides a way to thwart those who, for whatever reason, are bent on destruction. There are many persons in congregations throughout the church who consciously or unconsciously are out to get the leader, the pastor. Left alone like sheep before wolves, pastors sometimes feel helpless to defend themselves. Here the support of a team can be invaluable.

A dedicated layperson recently sent me a copy of a news article that reviewed a new book titled, *Clergy Killers, Guidance for Pastors and Congregations Under Attack.* The author, Reverend G. Lloyd Rediger, a Presbyterian pastor, has observed the sharp rise in the number of clergy being fired. He sees a root cause as people who make a practice of attacking pastors. The worst of these, he says, are people who have given themselves over to evil. According to Reverend Rediger, "They sabotage. They abuse. They are out to get someone, and it's usually the pastor standing there with a target on his or her chest." If this were to happen in a congregation where partners in ministry was in operation, lay members of the team would support the pastor and confront the destructive behavior.

Looking for loving intentions does not ignore the fact that evil intentions also exist. Certainly leadership team members selected because of their commitment to Christ and to the vision of the church will not act intentionally in a destructive way. But in nearly every congregation there are some who will.

Jesus emphasized the importance of acknowledging loving intentions when he was visiting in the home of Mary and Martha (John 12:1-18). Mary broke a box of costly ointment and anointed Jesus' feet. She was soundly criticized by the disciples, particularly Judas. The ointment could have been sold and the money given to the poor. Jesus pointed out her loving intentions, which tempered the reaction of Mary's critics. (See also Matthew 26:6-13.)

The critics of Jesus often accused him of being driven by evil intentions and motives (Luke 11:14-15). He knew what it meant to be misunderstood. He has called us to give others the benefit of the doubt and to look for positive motives before becoming overly critical. Evil is real, but we must be careful in attributing evil intentions to those whose behavior we may not understand. Leading from the heart means looking for loving intentions before we jump to conclusions.

Tell Me the Truth with Compassion

Paul exhorts us in Ephesians 4 to speak the truth in love. John also encourages us in his second epistle not to separate truth and love. The last of the HEART principles, *"Tell me the truth with compassion,"* affirms the unspoken request we receive from one another to share the truth and do so in a loving and compassionate way.

As Christians we are called upon to demonstrate Christian love in our actions and behavior toward others; that is, *everyone.* We are to be kind, compassionate, and forgiving, demonstrating in our relationships with others all the fruits of the Spirit. We are called to be perfect in love and, yet, most of us are painfully aware at times that we behave in unloving and noncaring ways. We must go to the Father for forgiveness time and time again.

On the other hand, there are times when we may be acting in an unloving manner unintentionally and unconsciously. The impact of our behavior often does not match our intentions; we are not congruent. At times like these we are dependent on one another to hear the truth about our behavior. Unless we become conscious or aware of the impact our behavior is having on others, we will continue to do these things. Have you ever been driving down the highway and, desiring to change lanes, you nearly pulled out in front of another car because they were in that area of your rearview mirror called the "blind spot"? We have blind spots with regard to our behavior, too. We need to have these areas brought to our attention by receiving what is known as *feedback.* Feedback in a guidance system is meant to keep a spacecraft on course. Feedback helps thermostats in our homes keep the temperature at the most comfortable level. Feedback can help us in our personal relationships to stay on course and correct offensive actions.

At some level we all want to know the truth about ourselves. Hundreds of inventories have been developed by psychologists and sociologists to help us gain insights into ourselves and our motivations, tendencies, characteristics, creativity, or lack of it. The list could go on and on. We are anxious to learn more about ourselves, and these inventories may help. However, feedback—gaining the perceptions of others who interact with us—is probably the most help-ful way to learn about ourselves.

If feedback is so powerful, why do we not receive more of it? The most obvious answer is that we don't ask for it! We go through life like a bowler rolling a ball down the alley hoping for a strike; but just before the ball hits the pins, a curtain drops. We don't know the score. We have tried our best and hoped for the best, but until the curtain is lifted, we just don't know. Receiving feedback on our behavior is the lifting of the curtain. Only others can tell us the impact of our behavior, and they are reluctant to do so for many rea-sons. We may be perceived as not being open to hearing feedback. The other person may be fearful that they might hurt our feelings, be misunderstood, or damage the rela-tionship. For these and many other reasons we are often reluctant to give one another feedback.

On the receiving end we may be afraid of what we will hear if we ask for feedback. It may hurt. To use the bowl-ing analogy again, we may find when the curtain is lifted that we did not get the strike we wanted but a terrible split or worse yet a gutter ball! And we have also received feed-back over the course of our lives that has been unconstruc-tive, punishing (intended to hurt), unsolicited, and delivered in an unloving manner. So, we fear negative feedback.

What we often overlook is that feedback is quite often positive! Many with whom you live and work have positive feedback they could share with you, but for some reason they fail to do so. Again, they may be concerned that you might be embarrassed or that they might feel a little uncom-fortable. Notice how often you get positive feedback from a third party. They give feedback to others hoping it will find its way to you!

Feedback can be low impact or high impact. Most of the feedback we receive on a regular basis is of the low-impact variety. Low-impact feedback lacks the oftentimes highly emotional characteristic that accompanies high-impact feed-back. In low-impact feedback we receive information about the perceptions of others concerning our behavior and its impact. We choose to accept or ignore the information based on our own perception of its usefulness. There is typically no demand or requirement that we change our behaviors.

High-impact feedback carries with it a request for change. This kind of feedback is often called confrontation. The same principle, "Tell me the truth with compassion," applies here as well; but because there is a request for change and an implicit or explicit dissatisfaction with current behavior, there is a possibility of an emotional charge. One may become defensive or angry or grow silent. This emotional aspect makes it extremely important that we learn how to confront one another when it becomes necessary and do so in a way that expresses love and concern and, hopefully, does not damage the relationship.

To summarize, feedback is extremely valuable. As we seek to grow into mature Christians and to go on to perfection, we need to know about our growing edges, blind spots, and flat sides. However, we do not always receive the feedback we need because we are reluctant to ask for it. Also, others may be reluctant to give us feedback because they are not sure we want it. We need to give one another permission to share feedback, both positive and negative. When we offer feedback, we need to learn how to tell the truth with compassion. Guidelines for giving and receiving low-impact feedback are described in Chapter 4.

Now we will discuss the steps needed in planning the high-impact feedback we call confrontation.

Confronting Team Members with Firmness and Compassion

When we work in teams, we inevitably experience conflict and disagreement. Others do or say things that cause us displeasure, ranging from confusion or mild irritation to outright rage. Whether these conflicts arise frequently or infrequently, we may be assured that when we deal with other human beings, they will eventually behave in ways that upset us; and we must somehow deal with the inner turmoil that results. We can choose either to harbor our distress or to confront an individual directly.

Some people are able to confront naturally and constructively, but most of us fear confrontation and attempt to avoid it. Or when we do confront, we do it poorly. When we harbor resentments, our relationships with those with whom we are in conflict will inevitably deteriorate. We may consciously avoid the other person, crossing the street when we see that individual coming toward us or looking away when we pass in the hall. Or, when avoiding that person is impossible, we may show our resentment in sarcastic remarks or verbal jabs that cause the other person to speculate about what is wrong. If that person is also afraid to confront, the situation becomes even more tense. Often the original issue may be forgotten; yet, two people will stay at each other's throats without really knowing why. Even more destructive is the situation where avoiding confrontation results in gossip. When we are afraid to confront others directly, we often talk about them to other people, thereby bringing them into the conflict.

We need to realize that conflicts are going to happen between people who work closely together or who live together, and the ability to confront others in constructive ways is critical. Conflict and confrontation are natural, but how we handle them can have either desirable or undesirable results. Our problem is learning to confront others when the situation demands it in such a way that the outcome is positive and the relationship remains intact. In this chapter we explore our fears about confronting others, outline some techniques designed to help in a confrontive situation, and point out some pitfalls to avoid.

Why Don't We Confront?

Few people really like to confront others. In fact, most of us find confrontation downright painful and avoid it whenever possible. We are afraid to confront for a number of reasons. Some of the more common are:

- insecurity about handling the confrontation and a fear of making the situation worse;
- fear that the other person will "drag one of our skeletons out of the closet" and counterconfront us;
- fear of losing the friendship and/or respect of an otherwise good colleague or friend;
- fear of retaliation by the other person.

We have all experienced these fears, and we also are painfully aware of instances in which one or more of these fears have been realized. However, the damage done by avoiding a confrontation or just ignoring the undesirable behavior will only lead to further deterioration in the relationship. As in the case of most fears, the reality is rarely as bad as we imagine.

How Do We Confront Firmly and Compassionately?

Fortunately, certain fairly simple techniques, which we all can learn, can reduce the probability of negative outcomes. The following principles can help you confront others constructively.

Ask for Time

Ask the person for time to meet. Be considerate of that person's schedule and estimate the time you think you will need. Make sure that you can talk privately and without interruption.

Set the Climate

State your intentions. Come to the point quickly and directly. Make sure that the purpose of the meeting and your intentions are clear. Do not keep the other person guessing about the agenda.

State your concerns or reservations. Let the other person know that you do not enjoy dealing with unpleasant issues; and if you are concerned that a behavior typical to that person might interfere with the discussion, express your anxiety. For example, if you are confronting someone who tends to become defensive and angry when criticized, you should address this issue directly by saying something like, "I'm afraid that when I tell you about this problem, you'll get angry and defensive. Then you won't be able to hear what I have to say, and we won't have a productive conversation."

State Your Case

Own your responsibility. Acknowledge that you may be a contributor to the problem. "I realize that I have often called meetings on very short notice, and you have had to adjust your schedule." But at the same time, let the other person know how his or her behavior affects you. "When you are late for meetings, I get irritated and feel discounted." Others need to know how you are reacting to their behavior.

Describe specifically the behavior you are confronting. Concentrate on the performance or behavior; do not evaluate or judge the person. An individual will accept "I get upset when you are late for meetings" more readily than "You are an irresponsible person." Avoid attributing motives to the person's behavior; no one really knows why another person behaves in a particular way. To say, "You are late because you like to irritate me," makes a speculation that can easily be denied and takes the force away from the main issue—habitual lateness.

Listen

Give 100 percent attention. Henry David Thoreau once wrote, "It takes two to speak the truth. One to speak and another to listen." Conflicts frequently result from poor communication and/or misunderstanding. Let the other person know that you are open to his or her response to your description of the problem. The other person may have misinterpreted your behavior and intentions. "I was late three times this week because I was putting the finishing touches on reports for the meeting. I wanted those reports to be complete and accurate, and I thought you would be pleased with my efforts." Look directly at the person; let the other person know that you are listening carefully to what is being said. As your personal style dictates, you might nod your head or interject some appropriate response.

Demonstrate understanding with listening checks. During and after the other's response, summarize what that person has said to make sure that you have heard what that individual intended to communicate. "Now let's see if I understand what you are telling me. You were late because you were putting the finishing touches on reports for the meeting and thought I would be pleased with their completeness and accuracy."

Negotiate

Request the specific behavioral changes you want. Do not leave any doubt in the other's mind about what you intend to occur. For example, you could say, "I would rather have you on time with complete reports; but if there must be a choice, I want you there on time."

Offer help. At this point you and the other person might negotiate changes in behavior. In some cases, you may need to make changes in your own behavior, such as giving more advance notice of meetings or meeting less frequently.

Describe positive and negative consequences. Particularly, describe the consequences of continued undesirable behavior. These consequences may be as mild as, "If this problem continues, our working relationship will suffer," or as severe as, "The ministry of our church will suffer if we cannot complete our tasks on time. The congregation is depending on all of us." On the other hand, it is also important to point out the benefits of changing that behavior: "If we can clear up this problem, we can make a great team and do truly excellent work."

Reach and Confirm Agreements

Restate the agreements you have reached. Be sure that you have been clearly understood and that you have clearly understood the other person. "Now let me be sure that I've got this right. I will announce meetings at least three days in advance; and you will be on time for those meetings, whether or not the report is completely fine-tuned. If you cannot come to the meeting with a complete report, you will let me know as early as possible before the meeting." Do not move away from this step until the other person confirms what you have said.

Establish follow-up. Arrange a specific time for the two of you to get together to evaluate how the new agreement is working. This step informs the other person that you are serious about wanting these changes; you are not just letting off steam, after which you will let the matter drop. A feedback session can also be a vehicle to reopen the issues if things have not changed or to recognize the accomplishment if they have.

Share Appreciations

Focus on the positive aspects of the relationship, and point out how your new understanding can further strengthen that association. Indeed, when two people are committed to maintaining a good relationship, confronting undesirable or unacceptable behavior can bring them closer together. The other person will be encouraged by the fact that you care enough about the relationship to remove or change anything that gets in the way. Ending on a positive note will almost always encourage behavioral changes.

These steps can assist your team members and others in confronting constructively, but even constructive confrontation is not necessarily enjoyable. Indeed, most confrontations are unpleasant, whether you are the initiator or the recipient. If you care at all about the other person and/or preserving the relationship, it is distressing to learn that something you have said or done has caused discomfort or anger.

Also, in order for confrontation to be helpful, both persons must be willing to listen and negotiate. In some situations and with some people, the outcome may be negative no matter how careful you are or how positive your attitude. But if both parties are willing to participate actively, a difficult experience can lead to interpersonal and spiritual development. This growth is the goal of confronting with firmness and compassion.

What Pitfalls Should You Avoid?

There are a couple of pitfalls. First of all, because confrontation is often perceived as an attack, the other person may become defensive. When such a situation occurs, do not argue or become defensive in return; doing so can lead to a stalemate. Stick with the issue; be specific and stay with that issue until the other person understands what is bothering you, why, and what you want changed.

Also, don't get off track or let yourself be derailed. If you are dealing with habitual lateness and how it affects you, do not let the other person change the subject or digress. Often you may be counterattacked: "I don't see how you can be upset because I am late for meetings. The meetings you chair always last too long." The long meeting issue may be a valid topic, but deal with it only after you have finished with the first issue. Better yet, make an appointment to discuss it at another time.

Defensiveness and derailment are common pitfalls that can undermine constructive confrontation. Be aware of them, and try to avoid them if at all possible.

Summary

Conflicts are a natural part of living and working in teams. Yet, most of us dislike facing negative situations and are scared off by our fears, even though avoiding necessary confrontations can cause deterioration in relationships. The steps outlined in this chapter can help you confront with firmness and compassion and, in the process, fulfill the fifth HEART principle, *"Tell me the truth with compassion."*

CHAPTER 3

Win-Lose Versus Win-Win

Another major covenant or ground rule for those who would be partners in ministry is to seek win-win solutions to problems, conflicts, or any other issues that may arise. A conscious decision to seek win-win solutions is essential because win-lose often seems inevitable.

We live in a culture where win-lose is pervasive. We see competition everywhere, with everyone wanting to be number one. Children compete for grades, for positions on teams, and for entrance into colleges. Adults compete for jobs. Our heroes are sports figures who play to win. Competition can be fun and is appropriate in many situations. At some point in a contest there needs to be a winner. However, for every winner there is also a loser or many losers. And when competition takes place within the family or the team, hard feelings, anger, jealousy, bitterness, and vengefulness often result. So, we must be careful not to carry appropriate win-lose behavior into situations where it is inappropriate.

People who feel like losers do not make good followers or team members. Win-lose behavior within the team results in the following consequences:

- Diverts time and energy from the main issues
- Obstructs the exploration of other alternatives
- Creates deadlocks
- Decreases sensitivity
- Arouses anger
- Interferes with listening
- Causes members to drop out

- Leaves losers resentful
- Inclines underdogs to sabotage
- Destroys trust and teamwork

Since competition and win-lose are so pervasive, how do we avoid it? To achieve win-win results, leaders must be willing and able to practice the following skills:

- Listening for understanding
- Speaking clearly and directly
- Seeking consensus
- Confronting
- Resolving conflicts
- Solving problems

Our leadership model would put voting way down on the list of problem-solving or decision-making techniques and emphasize instead dialogue and persuasion. Every time a vote is taken and the vote is not unanimous, we create losers. Losers do not make effective team members. Win-lose produces resentments, shuts down openness, drives disagreements underground, becomes the basis for factions and disharmony, and tempts the underdogs to sabotage. These and many other negative behaviors manifest themselves in a win-lose environment. Only a commitment to taking the time and making the effort to seek win-win solutions can avoid these destructive behaviors.

Recognizing and Dealing with Conflict

When human beings work closely together, conflicts or disagreements are bound to arise. Conflicting views can be constructive; they can help us look for new options or solutions that are better than those we have been producing. So, the first step is to view conflict as constructive.

It is important to take the time to listen carefully to all

points of view. Encourage everyone to speak out and then give evidence that each has been heard. Explain all the options and possibilities. Strive for consensus. Consensus means that all parties involved have been heard and the group has arrived at substantial agreement. All may not be equally excited about the solution, but no one feels discounted. Even if consensus cannot be reached, it is important to take enough time to try for it. If a decision does not go the way I would wish, I may not like it, but if I have had an opportunity to express my views openly and have been heard and not put down, I will not go away feeling like a loser. I am still a member of the team.

On those occasions when conflicts arise and win-lose attitudes and behaviors are present, the following model can help us move through this "minefield" and, hopefully, find a win-win solution. There are no guarantees; it is, however, a process that can work in many situations.

Step 1: Become Aware

To avoid a win-lose situation, the first step is to recognize that one exists. Change cannot occur without awareness of the current reality.

How do you recognize a win-lose situation? That depends on whether you are on the winning or the losing end. The winner can sometimes notice the discomfort or distress of the other person; at other times, he or she can become aware of a feeling of aggression or triumph blossoming inside.

From either the winning or the losing perspective, all hope of catching a win-lose before it has done damage and transforming it to a win-win depends on the awareness that, right now, a win-lose is in progress.

Step 2: Share Awareness

Once you realize that you are in a win-lose situation, the second step is to ensure that both parties are made aware.

When you are on the losing end, you might say something like these statements:

"I'm feeling uncomfortable. Can we slow down a minute?"

"It seems like this is a good deal for you, but it surely isn't for me."

While you are sharing your dissatisfaction, you must pay careful attention to the response. Here are examples of some positive responses you, the loser, might encounter:

"I didn't realize you were feeling that way. What can we do to make this a good deal for you, too?"

"I wasn't aware that this assignment would involve so many components. Let's discuss how we can split up the tasks to make it fair for both of us."

With responses like these, the process can proceed with the identification of each party's needs.

On the winning end, sharing awareness might sound like this:

"I'm concerned that this isn't a good deal for you."

"I'm getting what I want here, and I'm concerned that you may not be getting what you want."

These questions serve to uncover what the other person might be feeling. If the potential loser can affirm convincingly that he or she is not feeling like a loser, the matter can be dropped. However, the other person may confirm your suspicion with something like:

"Well, now that you mention it, I am feeling a bit uncomfortable with the situation."

"Thank you for asking. I don't feel comfortable being totally responsible for the whole program; I would really appreciate your help."

If this happens, the process can proceed with the identification of each party's needs. Or, you, the loser, might encounter a negative response such as:

"You always think you're getting the short end of the deal."

"You shouldn't feel that way because...."

"I think if you will reconsider, you will agree with me that...."

If this happens, you should inform the perpetrator that the inflicting of a win-lose will carry consequences.

What are the consequences of persevering with a win-lose even after the situation has been clearly identified? The degree of the consequence will depend upon a number of variables: the extent of the anticipated "loss," the importance of the relationship, and the relative position of each person, to name a few.

One way to halt would-be perpetrators in their tracks is to be explicit about these consequences:

"If you don't allow me the opportunity to contribute, some good ideas may be overlooked."

"If you are unwilling to give me positive feedback when I've done something well, eventually I will try to find a job where I am appreciated."

The consequences may be large or small, but letting people know what might happen gives them a chance to rethink and reconsider their positions. Frequently, it can nudge the win-lose perpetrator back to a more collaborative attitude. If this does not happen, at least you have given fair warning of the forthcoming consequences.

The important common point of these examples is to send an unmistakable signal that you have identified a win-lose. After this is done, it is critical to be quiet and listen carefully to the other person's response. Needless to say, the consequences presented should never be a bluff. If they are and the bluff is called, the bluffer will have succeeded only in destroying his or her own credibility. The goal of sharing consequences is to get the other person to make a more serious effort toward finding a common goal.

Step 3: Identify Needs

After you have identified and shared the win-lose situation, the third step is to identify needs. You might ask, "Why is this the next step?" The answer is that frequently people may differ on strategies or tactics but have an underlying unity of purpose. If the fact of their basic alignment on purpose can be established, they will be able to proceed from there as allies rather than adversaries. They can then pursue a solution that will serve their common purpose.

Step 4: Explore Alternatives

In any problem-solving effort, the chances of a high-quality solution emerging are generally enhanced in proportion to the quality of alternatives identified. The fourth step in getting to win-win, therefore, is to generate as many alternatives as possible.

There are at least three ways to do this: brainstorming, combining ideas, and lateral thinking. "Brainstorming" involves listing all conceivable alternatives with no evaluation or judgment offered as to their possible usefulness. The goal of brainstorming is sheer quantity with unusual, or even unorthodox, ideas welcomed for their contribution to creativity.

"Combining ideas" means taking elements of various alternatives and putting them together in new ways.

"Lateral thinking" is a term employed to describe a wide variety of creative techniques. It is characterized by the use of the right hemisphere of the brain and by structures that require nonlinear, nonsequential (hence, "lateral") associations of objects or ideas. In addition to being a technique for generating alternatives, lateral thinking qualifies as a separate skill area.

Step 5: Reach Agreement

The fifth and final step is reaching agreement on a plan or course of action. A set of alternatives having been identified, there are three ways of arriving at a decision that incorporates at least some of the interests and concerns of both parties: compromise, rotating bliss, and creative blend.

In a *compromise*, everyone comes away with a part of what he or she wanted, or "half a loaf."

In a *rotating bliss* solution, everyone gets all of what he or she wants, but only part of the time.

A third type of negotiated agreement is called a *creative blend*. It represents a true win-win in which everyone gets all of what he or she wants. How is that possible? Here is how it works. Imagine that a husband and wife are arguing about where to spend their vacation. Husband insists "the mountains"; wife is adamant on "the seashore." The argument becomes heated. Where is the win-win in that situation? The answer is that people often speak in metaphors, and behind those metaphors are irreducible elements. Frequently, while the metaphors may conflict, the elements can be harmonized.

In our domestic squabble, suppose the husband is asked what he likes about the mountains. He answers, "Serenity, peace and quiet, beautiful scenery." The wife is then asked what she likes about the seashore. She responds, "The beach, swimming, sunbathing." It just so happens that there is a lake in upstate New York that combines all elements—serenity, scenery, and a beautiful beach.

By interviewing the couple, it was possible to identify the irreducible elements that they really wanted and help them find a solution that gave both all of what they wanted—a true win-win resolution. Creative blends are possible far more often than they are found or sought.

Win-Win in the Early Church

Almost from the beginning the early church in Jerusalem experienced win-lose situations and coped with them successfully. In Acts 6 we find some of the widows of Greek disciples complaining that the Hebrew widows were receiving preferential treatment. This could have developed into a serious confrontation. However, the apostles took the matter seriously and appointed seven disciples to look after the distributions to all the widows. It is interesting to note in Acts 6:3 (RSV) that the freedom to choose the seven was given to the group as a whole with the only stipulation being that the men be "of good repute, full of the Spirit and of wisdom." When these were chosen, the apostles formally appointed them to their new duties (Acts 6:6). They achieved a win-win solution. The apostles were happy to be relieved of the responsibility and the people were delighted with the choice of personnel. As a result of this process, we read in verse 7, "The word of God increased; and the number of the disciples multiplied greatly in Jerusalem..." (RSV).

An even more serious situation arose and is recorded in Acts 15. Paul and Barnabas had great success in preaching the gospel to the Gentiles. Many were converted, baptized in the faith, and became a part of the small churches that arose all over Asia Minor. However, a serious question arose: Should these Gentile converts be circumcised? Many believers, especially in Jerusalem, saw Christianity as a continuation and fulfillment of the Jewish tradition. It was assumed that new converts would be circumcised in keeping with tradition dating back to Abraham.

Paul saw no need to circumcise Gentile converts. That was an issue that could easily have split the young church. It was a win-lose situation that could easily have become a lose/lose. It is hard to imagine what would have happened to Christianity had these two factions failed to resolve their differences. But, thank God, they did! They settled on a compromise of sorts that left all feeling like winners.

Notice how the process worked. Paul and Barnabas were received warmly by the brethren in Jerusalem (no "make-wrongs"—HEART principle #2), and the apostles and elders listened to them (HEART principle #1) as recorded in Acts 15:4. Then there was open disagreement (verse 5). They spent much time in debate (no quick vote). Then the leaders stood and suggested a direction and took a stand. First, Peter spoke (verses 7-11). They all listened carefully again to Paul and Barnabas (verse 12). Then James proposed a win-win solution (verses 13-21). The solution was accepted by all the apostles and elders; and when the solution was presented to the brethen in Antioch, they rejoiced (verse 31). After this, the whole church was enabled to continue to grow in peace.

Unfortunately, and in order to be fair, win-win solutions do not always work out the way we desire. In the next few verses of Acts 15, we find Paul and Barnabas embroiled in a heated disagreement over John Mark. Paul did not want to take him on the next missionary journey; Barnabas did. The only solution was for Barnabas to take John Mark and go off without Paul. Paul, in turn, took Silas and went his separate way (verses 36-41).

Summary

Getting from win-lose to win-win does not happen automatically. It requires a personal commitment to a win-win way of dealing with people and a desire to build relationships—leaving winners rather than losers in your wake. By following the five steps outlined above, win-win solutions can be achieved far more frequently than people imagine. Instead of being at the mercy of seductive win-lose situations, you can recognize them, manage them, and transform them into win-win solutions. Such an attitude allows you to be a winner and to create winners. In addition, this attitude benefits the church as a whole by improving the work climate, by improving teamwork, and by remarkably increasing the creativity that ultimately fuels every congregation.

CHAPTER 4

Trust and Team Building

One of the five major covenants or ground rules among leadership team members is that they will keep their agreements and be open and honest in their communications. In this chapter we will describe how trust and teamwork are developed, critical essentials for working as partners in ministry.

Trust Building

Partners in Ministry requires that clergy and laity in each congregation work as a team, providing effective leadership to the church. For effective teamwork each member must develop a high level of trust in each of the other members. Therefore, one of the primary covenants or ground rules is that all team members keep their agreements and are open and honest in their communications with one another.

Trust is the glue that holds meaningful relationships together, be they family, friend, marriage partner, coworker, or business associate. Trust is often slow to develop and can be destroyed in a heartbeat. Like Humpty Dumpty, it is difficult to put trust back together after it has been broken or betrayed.

If we trust one another, we will listen to one another, consider the other's thoughts and ideas, take a risk with them. Our willingness to take risks together is at the heart of effective team leadership. This is especially essential in the environment within which the church exists today. Many of the old ways of doing things are only effective with old-timers!

Change is taking place all around us; and even though the gospel never changes, our ways of presenting the gospel must change if we are to reach the lost, lonely, and alienated in our culture. This calls for thinking creatively; developing new models of worship, evangelism, and mission outreach; and taking risks.

How do we develop the trust that will allow us to take risks? The following model indicates how trust is developed in relationships.

TRUST MODEL

RISK
| TRUST |
| OPENNESS |
| CREDIBILITY |
| TEAMWORK BY AGREEMENT |

As the model indicates, trust is the result of a particular series of actions—actions that each of us controls for ourselves. The foundation of trust begins with making and keeping agreements. The process works in the following way.

Making and keeping clear, specific agreements with others will build your credibility with them; they will learn that they can depend on you. Others may like or dislike you, but they will know that you do what you say you will do and that you "keep your word." In turn, high levels of credibility lead to more openness—the willingness to share honestly and candidly. Furthermore, contrary to popular opinion, openness *precedes* and builds trust. Think for a minute: How many truly trusting relationships do you have with really closed people? Openness is, in many respects, a prerequisite condition for trust. So, the way to safer risk taking is to make and keep agreements, which leads to credibility, fosters openness, develops trust. The foundation is based on agreements.

Making Agreements

Perhaps the simplest and most surefire way to build credibility with others and to increase your effectiveness is by making and keeping clear, specific agreements with others and by getting others to make clear agreements with you. It is simple and so true, but it is something that many of us fail to do with any regularity. Recently a study of twenty-one high potential executives who were terminated or made to retire early from their companies was released by the Center for Creative Leadership in Greensboro, North Carolina. This study showed that the one universal character flaw that inevitably led to downfall was not doing something that was promised. The lack of clear agreements is currently one of the major sources of misunderstanding and irritation between people. Think about how many relationships have soured because of disappointment over an unfulfilled expectation on one side or the other. Frequently, unclear or broken agreements have been the cause.

The good news is that the situation can be remedied with relative ease. The technique of making and keeping clear agreements is easy to learn and has almost universal applicability. You can use it with peers, bosses, subordinates, friends, and family. All you have to do is follow the four ground rules below.

1. Make Only Agreements You Intend to Keep

Make only those agreements you are capable of keeping and fully *intend* to keep. Without thinking about the consequences, many people make agreements they do not intend to keep. Some people make agreements without realizing it; others make agreements they have no intention of keeping under the banner of "politeness"; and some people make agreements to temporarily get themselves out of "sticky" situations.

There is an old saying that indicates "what goes around comes around." Related to agreements, it means that agreements (however small or trivial) we make and don't intend to keep come back to haunt us with the loss of our credibility. Our credibility is not something to be taken lightly.

2. Avoid Making or Accepting "Fuzzy" Agreements

A second ground rule is to make and accept only clear, specific, firm agreements. When you agree to do something, make sure you and the other party know exactly what you are agreeing to do and when. Anything less than total clarity leaves room for misunderstanding and someone's being surprised. Often the result of such surprises is the loss of credibility.

On the other side of the coin, don't allow other people to make fuzzy agreements with you. Allowing others to make vague agreements often ends up with your being disappointed and their losing credibility. How can you keep other people from making "fuzzy" agreements? Question them to the void. If someone says, "I'll call you on this," ask, "When will you call? What day will you call? What time will you call?" If you get answers to these questions, you can agree to be there when the person calls.

Sometimes people make vague agreements to leave themselves an "out" if things don't go well; or they make vague, halfhearted agreements because they don't intend to keep them. In such cases, you can politely ask, "Do you fully intend to do this?" This has the effect of getting the person to commit one way or the other. One simple thing that will improve our effectiveness is to require clear agreements from others.

3. Give Earliest Notice When Agreements Cannot Be Kept

It is common courtesy that the other person be notified as *early* as possible when an agreement cannot be kept. Even with the best intentions and hard work, not all agreements can be kept; after all, we are all only human. When this happens, it will preserve your credibility if you let the other person know quickly. Early notification is better than a broken agreement. While all of us know this, it is easy to procrastinate on this type of bad news. When we do, we succeed only in delaying and worsening the inevitable.

4. "Clean Up" Broken Agreements

No matter how good our intentions, there will occasionally be times when agreements are not kept for whatever reason. When you break an agreement, be sure to talk to the person with whom you had the agreement. It is a simple matter to tell the person that you "blew it" and ask for forgiveness.

SUMMARY

We can be successful as a church when both lay and clerical leaders trust one another enough to work together effectively. This trust is built over time and is based on a foundation of credibility. We establish our credibility by making and keeping agreements with one another. We must protect our credibility at all costs. As people who worship and serve a God who keeps his word, we must keep our word. The world is watching. We need to be known as the people who keep their word. Our goal should be to achieve the level of credibility related by a woman talking about her father.

The father worked long hours and had often missed her school activities. When the daughter joined the high school band, he promised to attend every game. He kept his promise until one night when his flight home from a business trip landed right at game time, fifty miles away from his daughter's school. Although she was disappointed, she understood why he couldn't be there. Imagine her surprise when her band marched onto the field at half-time, and she happened to look up to see her father standing outside the fence in the pouring rain, just in time to see her perform! Looking back now, she realizes this was one of many times her father proved he was a man true to his word.

Team Building

Before we can explain how effective teams are developed, we must understand the meaning of "team." Sometimes groups of people are put together and instructed to work as a team when each person has a different agenda. "Team" implies that all members are committed to the same vision or mission. Obviously, and, hopefully, each member will have different ideas about how to accomplish the mission, but there is essential agreement among all on what constitutes the objective. Again, in a team all are active players and accept responsibility for the success or failure of any endeavor. When team members have agreed upon a course of action, all speak with the same voice and support any member who may come under fire or face opposition or criticism.

Teamwork like this does not just happen. It is the result of conscious effort. As we observed earlier, trust results from openness. Being honest and open with one another is essential. It implies getting to know one another and experiencing a degree of intimacy that goes beyond casual acquaintance. When openness is mutual, we develop a bond with one another.

Teams are composed of a series of complex one-on-one relationships:

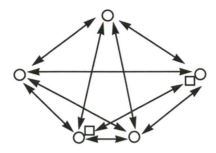

In teams individual relationships are important and need to be nurtured. How do we do this? There are two primary ways to develop a meaningful relationship with another team member: (1) self-disclosure and (2) giving and receiving feedback.

A Model of Communication

The simple model in Figure 1 helps illustrate the importance of both of these skill sets. In all forms of communication, there are both a sender and a receiver. All people communicate through a filter commonly called their "frame of reference." This frame of reference is comprised of the mixture of the person's past experiences and present state of affairs. It is the person's frame of reference that determines how the person communicates to others and how others' messages are interpreted.

Figure 1

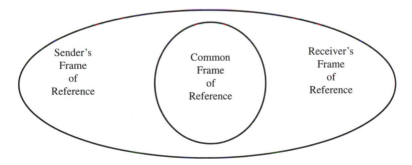

The problem is that people can communicate effectively only within their common frame of reference. And because everyone is unique, no two people have frames of reference that are exactly the same. Think about it for a minute. Can you communicate more effectively with someone you know well and who knows you well or with someone you know little about? The larger the common frame of reference between any two people, the more likely it is that they can communicate well. Said another way, the more we know about ourselves and one another, the better we can communicate.

It is through giving and receiving feedback and through self-disclosure that people enlarge their common frames of reference. The Johari Window Model, developed by Joseph Luft and Harry Ingham, helps illustrate how feedback and disclosure affect communication and relationships.

The Johari Window

The Johari Window in Figure 2 is essentially a communication window through which we give and receive information about ourselves and others. The left-hand column represents information that you know about yourself, while the right-hand column represents information that you do not know about yourself. The top row refers to things that others know about you, while the bottom row represents things that others do not know about you. Looked at in this way, there are four different panes (categories of information) in the window.

Figure 2

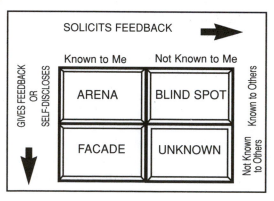

1. Arena

The arena is the information about us that is common and public. It represents the things that we know about ourselves and that others also know. Our arena is different for each person with whom we communicate.

The arena represents the common frames of reference mentioned. Thus, the size of the arena determines our potential for effective communication. The larger our arena is with a person, the more effectively we can communicate with that person.

2. Facade

The second category of information is the facade. This pane in the window represents information we know about ourselves that others do not know. It is information we have hidden from, or at least have not shared with, other people. Just as the size of the arena differs with different people, so does the size of the facade. Some people know a lot about us, and others know very little about us.

Everyone has a facade; it is the size of the facade that makes a difference. Moving information from the facade into the arena (letting people know more about us) increases our potential for effective communication.

3. Blind Spot

A third pane in the window is the blind spot. It represents things others know about us that we do not know. It may seem strange, but other people always know things about us that we are not aware of—perceptions picked up from our mannerisms, habits, and body language. We are often unaware of how others see us or of their opinions of us. As with the arena and the facade, the blind spot varies in size.

We all have a blind spot. There is no one who knows all of the things about himself or herself that any other person knows. Reducing the blind spot—finding out about ourselves what others already know—increases the arena and, therefore, increases the potential for effective communication.

4. Unknown

The fourth category in the window is the unknown—things we don't know about ourselves or one another. Some examples might be undiscovered talents, latent abilities, forgotten memories, etc. Some things in this category we may learn in the future about ourselves, and some things we may never realize.

If there were an ideal window, it would have a large, well-balanced arena. The size of the arena is important, and so is its shape. We can enlarge the arena by reducing any or all of the other three panes, but focusing on only one of these processes produces an unbalanced window. Communication effectiveness is limited because others see our behavior as inconsistent. We either give and do not receive, or we receive and do not give to others.

Self-Disclosure and Feedback

It is probably obvious by now that self-disclosure and feedback are the processes that determine the size and shape of the arena.

Self-Disclosure

Self-disclosure is the process of moving information from the facade into the arena. It involves allowing the other person to know more about who and what we are. Giving others feedback is another way of self-disclosing. If I give you my perception of you, I have, in the process, decreased your blind spot, decreased my facade, and increased our arena. Thus, self-disclosure is a way to increase the common frame of reference.

If anything, self-disclosure is probably riskier for most people than receiving feedback. As one person put it, "If I tell you who I am, that's all I have to give; and you may not like it." Even if it is not actually risky, self-disclosure is often a little scary. We generally wait until we can trust the other person before we feel comfortable enough to share significant things about ourselves. One prominent authority believes that, in this respect, we have the cart before the horse. We wait until we can trust the other person before we risk much significant sharing. But what will build the trust? In his book, *Self-Disclosure* (Wiley-Interscience, 1971), Sidney Jourard states his belief that self-disclosure precedes and builds trust in relationships. Rather than wait for the trust to develop, we can build it with appropriate self-disclosure. It works because as we trust others, they begin to trust us; as the process continues, trust builds to higher and higher levels.

The key to building trust through self-disclosure is the word *appropriate*. Appropriate self-disclosure has several dimensions. Appropriate self-disclosure means taking a moderate risk. It would be naive and dangerous to share deeply personal things before "testing the water" with less risky sharing. After all, building trust in relationships is an ongoing process, not a one-shot affair.

Appropriate self-disclosure is also relevant to the relationship, so what is shared needs to have some relevance to the relationship. Indiscriminate disclosure can damage rather than build relationships.

Appropriate self-disclosure also takes into consideration the needs of the other person. People have different thresholds for disclosing and for allowing others to confide in them. What we share may be only a minor jeopardy for us, but it could be very risky for the person hearing it. So, we must be sensitive to the other person. The general rule in disclosure is to slightly stretch ourselves and the other person with what we share.

In summary, self-disclosure enables us to increase our communication skills and build trust in our relationships. Thus, it is an important interpersonal skill that we need in order to work effectively with others and to develop teamwork.

Jesus was extremely open with his disciples about who he was (John 14:8-10). His mission was to reveal the heart of God. He was the Word made flesh. He advocated openness in his followers. Jesus also had a way of penetrating the facades of others.

Now let's look at the other skill set essential for effective team building—giving and receiving feedback.

Giving and Receiving Feedback

Giving and receiving helpful feedback is an essential team skill. It is one of the primary ways you help team members improve, and it's one of the primary ways your team members help you improve. While feedback is essential for effective teamwork, it must be given and received in the right way.

Feedback can be helpful or destructive. Giving and receiving feedback is simply a sharing of information in a particular way, so that it will have the highest likelihood of being truly helpful or constructive.

Feedback

Here are some things you can do to make the feedback you *give* helpful.

Before you give anyone helpful feedback, be sure to check with yourself to see if your intention is truly to be helpful to the person. This is an application of the principle, "Tell me the truth with compassion." If your motivation is to help the other person, your truth is more likely to be compassionate. It is sometimes easy to fall into the trap of giving another person feedback to make ourselves look good, to appear more intelligent than the person with whom we are interacting, or to hurt or embarrass the other person. If your intention is to help the other person, there is a much greater likelihood that your feedback will be heard.

In order for feedback to be helpful, it must be heard. Feedback is most likely to be heard if it has been requested. There will be times when feedback may be needed when it has not been requested. One way to handle that is to let the other person know you have some feedback for them and ask if they are open to hearing it.

The feedback should deal with a behavior the person can do something about if they choose to do so. To tell a person that he or she is too short is not very helpful since there is little any of us can do about our height. Therefore, feedback should deal with something a person says or does since the person can change these things as a result of hearing your feedback.

Feedback should deal with specific behaviors rather than generalities. For example, to tell someone that they are indifferent is not very helpful. It doesn't identify what the person is doing that makes you think he or she is indifferent. A more specific statement would be, "When you don't attend our meetings, I think you don't care." Then if the person wants you to think he or she cares about the work, they will understand the necessity of attending the meetings.

Helpful feedback should describe behavior, not evaluate it. For example, "When you don't finish your assignments on time, I think you don't care about your work," as opposed to, "Your indifference makes me think you don't care about our church." The first example describes a behavior—not finishing an assignment. The second example evaluates the person by calling them indifferent. Feedback that is evaluative, rather than descriptive, will probably be seen as a make-wrong.

After describing a specific behavior, let the person know what the behavior makes you think or how you feel when they behave in that way. For example, "When you don't attend our meetings, I think you don't care about our work." Or, "When you don't show up, I get very angry."

In order to be most helpful, feedback should be well timed. It should be given as soon as possible after the behavior occurs, or the most recent example of the behavior should be used. Something that happened today is more likely to be remembered than something that happened last week, last month, or last year. Another aspect of timing is the issue of privacy. People may be more receptive to hearing certain feedback in private rather than in public. In addition to this, some feedback is simply not appropriate given in public.

Feedback should be checked to see if the receiver understood the message the way the sender intended it to be understood. The message may be distorted by either the sender or the receiver. A way to check to see if this has happened is to ask the person to paraphrase back to you what they heard because you're not sure you have made yourself clear. This gives both of you a chance to clear up any misunderstandings.

The receiver of the feedback should be encouraged to *check with other people* to find out if only one person thinks or feels a certain way about their behavior, or if those thoughts and feelings are shared by other people. Feedback is more likely to be heard and understood if it is checked with others. Other people may also be able to provide some more examples of behavior for the person to consider.

In giving feedback remember to

- check to be sure your intentions are to be truly helpful;
- make sure the person is open to hearing the feedback;
- focus on changeable behavior;
- be specific;
- be nonjudgmental;
- time the giving of the feedback well;
- check for understanding.

As already stated, asking for and receiving helpful feedback are important for increasing your effectiveness, both personally and professionally. Many of the criteria that apply to giving constructive feedback also apply to asking for constructive feedback.

When you would like to get someone's thoughts and feelings about something you have said or done, the following guidelines will help ensure that the information you *receive* will be helpful to you.

Be specific in describing the behavior about which you want feedback. Rather than saying, "Go ahead and tell me what's wrong with me," ask for the person's thoughts and feelings about a specific thing you said or did. For example, "How did you feel when I told you I didn't have time to look at any new projects?"

Listen for understanding. Since you have asked for the person's feedback, *try very hard not to act defensively*. Instead, summarize your understanding of the feedback so that both you and the sender will be sure that the message was not distorted by either of you.

Avoid justifying your behavior and/or becoming defensive. Let the sender know your thoughts and feelings about the feedback you have received. Was it helpful to you? How are you feeling about what you have heard? How are you feeling toward the sender of the feedback now?

Confirm the feedback you have received with others when possible. If the feedback is totally inconsistent with the way you perceive yourself and your behavior, check with others you trust. Ask them how they see you. Refrain from asking the questions in such a way that you will hear only what you want to hear, but give them permission to be open and honest with you.

Respond to the person who gives you feedback. One who is willing to give you feedback, not knowing how you will receive it, is giving you a gift. Be sure to thank them for this gift. Only then will you be leaving the door open to gain further insights as to how others perceive you, and only then can you grow as a leader.

To receive feedback:

- Ask. Be specific.
- Listen.
- Avoid justifying your behavior and/or becoming defensive.
- Confirm with others when possible.
- Respond.

Feedback is simply additional information about a person's behavior. It is information that helps you and others determine if your behavior has the effect you intended it to have.

How do people grow and develop? Some growth is built in through our genetic makeup. We are programmed with regard to our height, skeletal structure, and muscular development. We all know this, and we are beginning to realize that with careful attention to nutrition and hygiene we can even have some influence on our genetic programming. We are not completely at the mercy of fate.

The same is true of our emotional and personality development. To a large extent we are the reflection of other people who have had a significant effect on our lives—parents, guardians, grandparents, teachers, ministers, friends. Some theories of personality development go so far as to state that by the time children reach five or six years of age, their basic personality or character structure is formed. This is a deterministic point of view that, at worst, gives people an excuse for their weaknesses and failures and, at best, gets in the way of motivation for change.

Any cursory study of the life histories of successful people indicates that with motivation and desire, and in many cases, help and encouragement from others, we can overcome negative childhood influences and significantly change our thinking and behavior as adults.

It is important to believe throughout our lives that we can continue to grow and change. If we do not believe this, we have no recourse but to surrender our destinies to fate or into the hands of others who do believe they can change and direct the course of their lives and the lives of others.

If we do believe that we can grow, change, and develop, it follows that others can also. This has major implications for churches, organizations, and teams. Team members now have increased responsibility for production and morale—*what* gets done and *how* it gets done. They also have the responsibility to discover, assess, and develop new talent and leadership to ensure the long-term success of the team. This responsibility, unfortunately, often gets overlooked or is given only leftover energy (if we have any left over).

Feedback is one of the most valuable and powerful tools we have to help one another grow and develop. One major indicator of a healthy team is the extent to which team members solicit and offer honest feedback in a spirit of being helpful.

Summary

In order to build trust and teamwork, we need to establish our credibility by keeping our agreements, being open with others through appropriate self-disclosure, and developing skill in giving and receiving feedback.

When we and other team members do these things consistently, we develop the trust necessary to take the risks we will inevitably be called upon to take in order to fulfill our ministry together.

CHAPTER 5

Responsibility for Results

An effective team is composed of members who take full responsibility for the results that are produced by the team and refuse to be seduced into blaming and justifying behavior. That is why one of the five ground rules or covenants among those who would be partners in ministry states that all team members assume 100 percent responsibility for the results that are produced and do not engage in blaming and justifying.

This is an extremely important ground rule. It goes against accepted norms of everyday behavior. We live in a culture where blaming and justifying are normal and perfectly acceptable. It is a necessity today to have liability insurance. It takes very little provocation at times to prompt people to sue one another in a court of law and be awarded large sums of money for any real and sometimes imagined injury. Many may remember the famous case of the woman who was burned when she spilled hot coffee on herself at a McDonald's restaurant. She sued the restaurant chain and was awarded millions in damages. Our culture is becoming more and more litigious. Our laws provide for just compensation when real damage has been done and this is right. However, the motivation for many is greed—to get something for nothing.

At the top levels of leadership in our nation, blaming and justifying are normal behavior. One suspects that the motivation for many Senate investigating committees is purely political rather than an attempt to redress wrongdoing. The media follow these hearings, so we all are exposed to accusations and counteraccusations and justification upon justification.

What is wrong with this behavior? Why get upset about it? It's human nature, isn't it? Adam and Eve started the process, and we are simply carrying on a grand tradition! Certainly, when unwanted results occur, it is appropriate to look for a cause or reason and, hopefully, make the proper corrections. However, so much of our time is spent in faultfinding and not in problem solving.

Blaming and justifying as ends in themselves can be extremely destructive. They can destroy personal relationships. When we are blamed for something, our typical response is to become defensive and counterattack. Escalating conflict results. We often find ourselves in win-lose situations that degenerate to lose-lose.

Blaming and justifying destroys effective teamwork as well. They cause members to be cautious, avoid risks, and watch what they say. Trust evaporates. Members are no longer open and honest with one another.

We pay a high price in terms of other negative results as well. For instance, nothing changes. When blaming and justifying become an end in themselves, the result is a dead end. The original situation or event does not change just because we have found a scapegoat or have successfully defended our own behavior. Years ago our national leaders engaged in what was called the Iran-Contra hearings. After months of testimony a large volume was published indicating that the results were inconclusive. We also were subjected to the Whitewater investigation. When the smoke cleared, we had the same result—no conclusion. In the meantime, valuable resources have been squandered in an attempt to find someone to blame. Again we must pursue and persecute serious wrongdoing even, or especially, at high levels of leadership. However, when the primary purpose is political, typically nothing of any value is accomplished and certainly nothing changes.

When we are focused on blaming and/or justifying, we are not looking for options to fix whatever needs fixing or to improve the process. To spend all our time trying to determine who left the barn door open leaves little time to determine how to round up the horses and make sure that it doesn't happen again! Yet, in the church we often spend hours in committee meetings diagnosing what has happened rather than strategizing more effective ways to accomplish our mission. Blaming may be more fun, and it certainly takes less effort; but if we don't look for better solutions to the problems and challenges we face, it is a waste of time.

In addition, blaming and justifying is disempowering. If I blame you for the negative results, I'm saying, in effect, that you had all the power in the situation. How can I hold you responsible if you were powerless to do anything about it? How can I blame you if I had the power to correct the situation? When we blame others, we give our power away. Power and responsibility go hand in hand. If I have the power to change things, then I can be held responsible. If I give up my power, it is easier to escape responsibility. This is a very dear price to pay to be able to blame. God has created us with many special gifts and abilities. We can dream, envision, and create. He has given us the power of choice, to decide what we will do or will not do. His greatest gift is the power of his Holy Spirit. With the power of the Holy Spirit, we can fulfill our purpose in life and bring others into his kingdom. No one can take this wonderful power away from us or rob us of our God-given abilities. We can only lose any or all of these by giving them away. What a tragedy it is to do this! Yet, when we blame and justify, we do just that. We deny our God-given gifts and abilities.

Finally, and most devastating of all, blaming and justifying, when developed into a lifestyle, result in victimhood. Victims lack any responsibility for their condition in life. No matter what happens, it is someone else's fault. They are helpless and powerless to change anything. They are lost. There is a certain comfort in being a victim. Victims escape blame. How can one blame a victim? They can criticize and pronounce judgment on anything and everything with impunity. Victims are not required to do anything, give anything. Victims deserve everything they get, and no gift can compensate for their victim-hood. We were not created to be *victims,* but *victors.*

One day Jesus was walking in the temple area and came upon the pool of Bethsaida. He saw a man who had been lying by the pool day in and day out for many years. Jesus engaged the man in conversation and found that friends carried him there each day where he hoped to be carried into the pool when it was "troubled," because then he could be healed. The first one in the pool when it was troubled would be healed, but he never made it first. He was a help-less victim of his circumstances. Jesus offered another solu-tion—to accept his gift of healing, walk away, and never come back. Fortunately, the man gave up the security and predictability of his victimhood and followed Jesus. Christ offers this healing and power to all of us. The opposite of victimhood is victory—victory in Jesus.

So, blaming and justifying is very tempting but lead to a dead end and cause alienation among ourselves and others as well as alienation from Christ and all he wants to do in our lives.

If we are to escape from these negative consequences of blaming and justifying, we must go back and take a look at our current understanding of responsibility. When we think of responsibility as shared, we open the door to all the neg-ative consequences stated above. Since we know we cannot control situations and other people, how else can we view responsibility?

The solution requires a new way of looking at responsi-bility. When unwanted results are occurring, *look at* the sit-uation *as though* are 100 percent responsible and others are 0 percent responsible.

On the surface this appears to be completely unreason-able, ridiculous, and unworkable. Hold on for a moment. Think of this as viewing a video designed to be seen through a set of three-dimensional lenses. Without the lens-es, the image appears flat—two dimensional. With the lenses, the picture seems to come alive and we are in the mid-dle of the action. When we view responsibility this way, we

96

- stop blaming and justifying.
- see options we could not see before.
- feel empowered to seek new solutions that may lead to more desired results.

Responsibility is our ability to respond; and since we have been created with a mind and free will, we can choose how we respond to any situation.

Consider this formula:

$$E + R = O$$

The **E** represents events, past or present, people, situations, etc. In most cases we have little or no control over the events that show up in our lives. The **R** represents our response to the events of life. If we choose to accept it, we are always in total control of our response to events. (If you're not in control, who is?) The **O** represents the outcome. Outcomes are largely the results of events plus our responses to events.

The way this formula typically works is as follows:

Event + Response = Outcome

Unwanted results	Blame and justify	Nothing changes
		Victimhood
		No options

The other way to look at responsibility might result in the following:

Event + Response = Outcome

Unwanted results	100% - 0%	No blaming
		No justifying
		Empowerment
		Options
		Creative solutions

We as leaders in the church have no excuse for living and acting like disempowered victims. We have available to us the power of God through the Holy Spirit. We can be empowered by God to create the desired results in the church, but it requires a new look at responsibility. It also requires the courage to stop blaming and justifying and to claim our ability to respond. By claiming the power and promises of God, we create the kingdom of God where we live, work, and worship. In Luke 5:17-26 we read about friends of a paralyzed man who did just that. They took 100 percent responsibility for seeing that their friend got to Jesus for healing by lowering their paralyzed friend through the roof. This was certainly unorthodox, somewhat risky (someone could get hurt), and perhaps even intrusive because Jesus was so busy. They did it anyway because they refused to be victims of circumstance.

Our Lord never allowed himself the luxury of feeling like a victim. He consciously and freely chose to endure a sinner's death in order that we sinners could be saved. He maintained a position of 100 percent responsibility and refused to blame or justify. He refused to respond to the abuse he received at the hands of Caiaphas and made it clear to Pilate who was in control (see Matthew 26:59-64; 27:11-14; John 18:33-37; 19:8-11).

Summary

Like the disciples and followers on the day of Pentecost, we have access to the power of the Holy Spirit that enables us to see visions, dream dreams, and participate with God in the creation of his church. We have the ability. Are we willing to respond? As partners in ministry, we covenant together and with God to avoid blaming and justifying and take responsibility for results.

Are You Able?

As with every good thing in life, there are both costs and benefits. The mother of James and John requested that her sons have honored seats in the coming kingdom of God (Matthew 20:20-23). Jesus reminded her of the cost and asked, "Are you able?"

All new ventures challenge both our willingness and our ability. Though Jesus' question was, "Are you able?" I think he was talking more about willingness than ability. Most of us have more ability than we are willing to use for God's kingdom.

With regard to PIM the laity need to answer some tough questions beginning with, "Are you willing to do what it takes?" What does it take?

Laity

For one thing it takes a firm belief in the process and a strong desire in our hearts to become a partner in ministry. It requires a willingness to be trained in necessary skills and a commitment to stay the course. It requires a dedicated life of prayer for the leadership of the church and an openness to listen and respond as God calls us into ever-expanding avenues of service. Are we willing to spend more time in prayer and service than ever before?

Are we as laity willing to put our finances where our faith is? When God opens new doors of ministry, will we be willing to open our purses to support the ministry? Are we willing to give more of our time and resources than we ever dreamed we would or could?

As Bonhoeffer affirmed, there is a cost associated with discipleship. Most of us have only given token obedience and not sacrifice. The time has come to truly put the kingdom of God first. This is the challenge to all of us who would be partners in ministry. As laity, are we willing and able? There are tremendous benefits to be experienced if we are willing to both count the cost and pay the price!

Clergy

Clergy, too, must weigh the costs and benefits of partners in ministry. This is a way of life, a new way of functioning and not simply a new program to push. Being partners in ministry calls for a new form of leadership; and once leaders go down this path, they will probably never want to go back.

This new form of leadership will allow us to expand our mission to the world around us because we have a team of persons equally committed. We can leverage our efforts. For one thing we may no longer need to attend every meeting, make every call, even preach every sermon! We can focus our time and energy on what counts by actually delegating authority and responsibility.

Long ago the greatest leader in the Old Testament (in our opinion), Moses, learned these lessons. Consider the incident recorded in Exodus 17:8-13. During the forty years in the wilderness the Hebrews faced many obstacles, not the least of which was hostile people who were determined to block their way or eliminate them altogether. One such group was led by Amalek. As the people prepared for battle, Moses engaged in delegation. Joshua was given the task of leading the soldiers in battle. Moses took a stand on top of a hill overlooking the action. Even here he took Aaron and Hur with him.

The story recounts when Moses held his arms high with the rod of God in his hand, the Hebrew people prevailed over Amalek. However, when Moses' arms grew weary and he lowered them, the people noticed and Amalek prevailed. When Aaron and Hur noticed this, they went to Moses' aid, held up his arms, and gave him a stone to sit upon. As a result, Joshua and the people mowed down Amalek.

This story is instructive for many reasons, but we want to focus here on Moses' leadership behavior. Both his instincts and necessity led him to delegate responsibilities. We see him expanding this practice in the next chapter following the counsel of his father-in-law, Jethro.

This is an extremely important point. Many clergy feel that to get the job done, they must do it themselves. Partners in Ministry seeks to correct this, but the clergy must also be willing to relinquish some control. Here is a price the clergy must pay to receive the benefit. As clergy, we must be willing to give up much of our hands-on behavior and micromanaging. Moses knew his strengths and limitations. He was a visionary and an inspirational leader, not a fighter. He didn't even go into the valley to get a closer look or to hold progress meetings with Joshua.

Pastors who are team leaders can devote more of their time to articulating the vision of the church. As Rick Warren tells us in *The Purpose Driven Church,* we must continually recast the vision; and as Lee Allen, a pastor in Alabama, stated recently, "If PIM is your vision for your church, you must consistently recast and restate that vision. This takes time, energy, and focus; but in the long run, it is well worth the investment." A willingness to delegate offers the clergy the time to focus on and hold up the vision as Moses held up the rod of God in the wilderness.

The partners in ministry team approach to leadership also allows the clergy an opportunity to inspire followers who are engaged in fulfilling their discipleship, not do the work for them. But this team approach requires that the clergy relinquish some control and trust that the Holy Spirit will work in the lives of his or her partners in ministry to accomplish the mission of the church.

So, delegating, sharing control and authority with followers, trusting, risking—these are some of the costs associated with PIM. It also requires for many of us a new model of leadership in which we focus on visionary, inspirational, and servant leadership. It also requires that we receive some training in functioning as a team leader. For some it may seem like starting over, and the price may seem too high. So, the questions for clergy, as well as laity, are: Are you able? Are you willing? Though Partners in Ministry may not be for everyone, we must be honest in our answers to these questions. Following are excerpts from a testimonial sent to us by Dr. David Jones, Pastor of First United Methodist Church, Borger, Texas:

> PIM training helped to curb a variety of potentially *destructive* behaviors and establish in their place a variety of potentially *constructive* behaviors. This is important because our church leaders considered leadership in the church to be a privilege and only desired potential leaders who exhibited that attitude. PIM helped infuse our church staff and governing board with joy, meaning, and satisfaction.
>
> Conflicts can be harmful and even destructive. They can cause individuals a great deal of pain and the community of faith immeasurable damage. At the same time, conflicts can be an opportunity for new insights, learning, and individual and congregational growth. Disagreements can illuminate a topic in helpful ways and can present solutions to problems that previously had not been seen. The successful resolution of conflict can also bind people together in a powerful way. We realize that our perspectives are limited, so we invited Dr. and Mrs. Trueblood to lead us in a three-day PIM workshop. In that workshop we practiced affirming one another, learned practical ways of enhancing our Christian community, the benefits of staying open to the viewpoints of others, the need to be sensitive to diversity, and the value of establishing common behavioral guidelines and expectations for all church leaders, whether laity or clergy.
>
> When the work of the Committee on Nominations and Personnel began in early fall of 1995, several committees were without leadership. For the first time in remembered history, leader vacancies in the church totaled 28 percent. *These positions remained vacant until after the PIM workshop in September 1996. Thanks in large part to the PIM workshop, all church leadership positions were filled with men and women who desired to serve in their areas. New leaders who had missed the training in September heard such great things about the PIM training that they began asking for PIM training a.s.a.p. Soon thereafter, the governing body of First UMC adopted a resolution prescribing that as soon as qualified trainers were available, PIM training would be a prerequisite*

for all new incoming church leaders. We now have three PIM trainers and a leadership workshop is being scheduled for February 1998. The Nominating Committee is now in the pleasant position of having people volunteer for leadership in the church. With established behavioral norms in place, and quality PIM training available, our experience is that people lose their hesitation to serve in church leadership roles.

During the PIM workshop several insights came to light:

- When I come into a new church assignment, I am coming into an already established congregation (a preexisting group). I don't make or break what God is doing in this congregation, I simply enter into dialogue with those who are already engaged in ministry to their community.

- Churches have an uncanny knack of outliving seminaries, pastors, and denominations. At best, as pastor I am first among equals. Partners in Ministry concepts help me better understand and work with this profound entity known as a congregation—this thing that is going to outlive me. The congregation is at the core of how faith is communicated, and the Partners in Ministry workshop enabled/enhanced the effectiveness of this ministry by helping us work more effectively together.

- The congregation needs leadership in order to be effective. It has been my experience that people who are involved in decision making within the church seem to gravitate toward the pastor. Partners in Ministry training and concepts have helped me and other congregation leaders to consider the pastor as first among equals.

- Partners in Ministry training encouraged me to listen for the stories because God seems to move his church through story and reveals truth in story form. Instead of imposing my individual vision upon the congregation, I am a better leader when I partner with lay leaders. Partnering in leadership leads me to a better understanding of what God is doing in and through this congregation. Only when I partner with other church leaders am I privileged to receive their stories—their

103

interpretations of where God is leading them. Only when I partner with them am I allowed by them and God to become part of the story, too.

PIM energized our congregation through the HEART principles. Through the hearing and understanding of our stories, mutual respect for another's interpretation, acknowledging greatness in one another through story, remembering to look for our loving intentions in telling our stories, and telling the truth in our stories with compassion, our people have been reenergized. Denominational stands and proclamations give us permission but no energy. Our HEART stories give us both energy and permission.

Have the HEART principles made us a conflict-free church? No. Since we are human, there is still a small degree of internal conflict, enough to make us alive. A church without internal conflict is not human—not alive. Periodically, we also experience some degree of external conflict. But that is okay, too, because a church without external conflict is not Christian. And even our conflicts are remembered in story form.

As a seminary-trained pastor with a doctor's degree, I thought I had a right to power. I felt that I had earned it. One church used a heartless method to harshly and painfully shock me from that delusion by excluding me. The next church (using the HEART principles of PIM) warmly shared their stories with me and invited me to be a full partner with them in ministry to our community. Guess which church I cherish. Both.

Part way through our PIM workshop, I became a little bit embarrassed that I would have to struggle with my clergy feelings in front of the laypersons who were my colleagues in leadership. I chose to be vulnerable, wondering if God would sustain me. If he did, maybe I could begin to open up more in front of the Sunday morning congregation. God came through for me and my leaders, and the whole congregation is becoming more trusting and open with one another. Whereas the former leaders of this traditional First Church use to say, "I've got the office. Follow me," we now say, "Thank you for loving me." PIM is helping us move from a cold structure to warm and caring relationships.

CONCLUSION

Partners in Ministry, as we have defined it, is just one attempt to save the soul of the church. This is a strong statement and, maybe for some, a bit arrogant. What we mean is to recapture the love and trust for one another, both clergy and laity, that will allow us to complete the work Christ has called us to accomplish in each of our communities to preach the gospel, to visit the sick and infirm, to care for the widows and orphans, to love the little children, to seek and to save the lost. This is what we mean by saving the soul of our church.

There are many things we can do. We can restructure our bureaucracy, shift people and funds around, eliminate some jurisdictions, engage in cost cutting. This could help. We can engage in a liturgical revival or teach people a "better" way to worship by bringing in contemporary music and worship services that appeal to the new generation we have chosen to call "X" (maybe because we do not know them). Doing any of these things might help.

However, if we are not careful, we may be guilty of the error made by the rich farmer in the parable Jesus told. He did a wise thing by building new and larger barns. This way grain would not be wasted and he might get a better price later on. But it was his soul that was at stake. All his other efforts seemed foolish and fruitless in the eyes of the Lord. We also remember Martha busily attending to the needs of her guests and the words our Lord spoke to her, "What is the one thing that is needful? It is to be about our Father's business." Wesley raised this concern over two hundred years ago when he wrote in a sermon called "Thoughts on Methodism" (1786), "I am not afraid that people called Methodist should cease to exist, but they should only exist as a dead sect, having the form of religion without the power."

Where does PIM fit in? I think Jim Lane in the laity address to General Conference may have said it best:

What does it mean to become "partners in ministry" in the twenty-first-century church? It means a place for service and ministry for everyone! A place where everyone is worthy and valued and has equal voice. It is a partnership that places far more value on your ability to see through "kingdom eyes" than it does your certificates, diplomas and credentials. Being partners in ministry values the "warm heart" and the "passion for souls" that not only is our heritage as people called Christians, but gives us our vision for the future. Partners in Ministry is not just another program for us to consider. It is in fact a "new way" for folks in ministry to work together in our great church. It is an attitude, an ethos, something that permeates how we "do church." Out of the understanding of Partners in Ministry, a new model for leadership in the church is emerging. This new model calls for sharing in ministry and leadership between the pastor and the local church laity. It is crucial for pastors and lay leadership to work in tandem as partners in ministry. This requires a deep level of trust, commitment, and communication on both sides. How can we foster more effective teams in ministry? Our vision is that each congregation within United Methodism will be equipped with the resources and skills to engage in a shared ministry for Christ—both within the Church and throughout the world. This shared ministry is focused on the primary task of the church and yoked with each church's own unique shared vision. A new millennium is dawning and many of us in the church are ready! God's Word through Isaac to us today is, "I am about to do a new thing: now it springs forth, do you not perceive it?" The clarion call to be "partners in ministry" is valid and urgent.